Till He Come

James Hall Brookes

SOJOURNER

PRESS

ISBN 978-1-960255-02-0 (Paperback)

ISBN 978 1 960255 03 7 (Epub)

Printed in the United States of America
Sojourner Press
Raleigh, NC
sojournerpress.org

For bulk, special sales, or ministry purchases, please contact us at sales@sojournerpress.org.

Contents

Introduction to the Revised Edition

James Hall Brookes (1830–1897) was an American Presbyterian pastor, Christian leader, and author. He served congregations in Ohio and Missouri for 43 years and became a leader in the Niagara Bible Conference. He was a premillennialist and is considered by many as one of the founding fathers of the dispensational movement in the United States. He was a prolific writer, producing over 200 books, booklets, tracts, and journal articles.

Till He Come was originally published in 1891, six years before Brookes' death. It is an extremely valuable resource due to the careful attention paid to the details of Scripture, and the clear articulation of premillennialism. Brookes wrote the book to counter the prevalent postmillennialism of his day, and since postmillennialism is currently on the rise again, Brookes' arguments find a welcome audience to the inquiring reader.

I have significantly updated the formatting and Scripture references in this revised edition so that the reader will be able to follow along more readily. I have also added a few comments in the footnotes to help explain some of Brookes' comments. As such, this revised edition provides the modern reader with another valuable resource for studying the second coming of Christ.

Peter Goeman, 2023
Raleigh, NC

Preface

It is the aim of this little book to set forth the truth of God concerning the second coming of His Son. No doubt there are a thousand who today accept the truth and are "looking for that blessed hope" where there was one twenty-five years ago. But there are thousands more who probably have never heard it mentioned. It has dropped out of the preaching and teaching of most men as completely as if it had no place in the inspired Scriptures.

It may be that the Holy Spirit will own the testimony here borne to awaken some of God's dear children to the study of a subject of vast practical importance. At all events, if they will read these few pages, they can see an outline of the faith held by those who heed the Master's command, "What I say unto you, I say unto all, Watch." And they can also see "a reason of the hope" that shines more brightly and beautifully, as we move on through increasing darkness and tempest and temptation "to meet the Lord in the air."

St. Louis, June, 1891

1

The Apostles' Teaching

Our risen Lord had appeared on many occasions to His disciples, "to whom He presented Himself living after his suffering, by many infallible proofs, being seen of them forty days, and speaking of the things pertaining to the Kingdom of God" (Acts 1:3). This naturally led them to ask of Him, "Lord, wilt Thou at this time restore again the Kingdom to Israel? And he said unto them, It is not for you to know the times or the seasons, which the Father hath placed in His own authority" (Acts 1:6–7). As Jews, familiar with their prophets, they expected the cessation of Gentile dominion, and the restoration of the Kingdom to Israel; and the Lord gave them no hint that their expectation was vain, but only that it was not for them to know the times or seasons, which, in the office work of redemption undertaken by the persons of the Godhead, specially fell under the authority of the Father.

Then followed the promise of the gift and power of the Holy Ghost, and the great commission:

> "Ye shall be witnesses unto me both in Jerusalem, and in all Judaea, and in Samaria, and unto the uttermost part of the earth. And when he had spoken these things, while they beheld, he was taken up; and a cloud received him out of their sight. And while they looked stedfastly toward heaven as he went up, behold, two men stood by them in white apparel; Which also said, Ye men of Galilee, why stand ye gazing up into heaven? this same Jesus, which is taken up from you into heaven, shall so come in like

manner as ye have seen him go into heaven. Then returned
they unto Jerusalem from the mount called Olivet, which
is from Jerusalem a sabbath day's journey" (Acts 1:8–12).

Luke adds in his Gospel, "They worshipped Him, and returned to
Jerusalem with great joy" (Luke 24:52).

We are not told who these two men were, but it is worthy of notice that
the same inspired writer mentions the appearing of two men in white at
two other momentous periods in the earthly history of our Lord. On the
mount of transfiguration, "as He prayed, the fashion of His countenance
was altered, and His raiment was white and glistening. And, behold,
there talked with Him two men, which were Moses and Elias[1]; who appeared in glory, and spake of His exodus which He should accomplish at
Jerusalem" (Luke 9:29–31). On the morning of the resurrection, when
the women went to the sepulchre to anoint the body of their crucified
Friend, "they found the stone rolled away from the sepulchre. And they
entered in, and found not the body of the Lord Jesus. And it came to
pass, as they were much perplexed thereabout, behold, two men stood
by them in shining garments: and as they were afraid, and bowed down
their faces to the earth, they said unto them, 'Why seek ye the living One
among the dead?'" (Luke 24:2–5).

It is not an improbable conjecture, therefore, that the same two men
in white or lustrous clothing who spoke of His exodus at Jerusalem, and
who heralded His exodus from the tomb, were also sent to proclaim
His second coming. Nor is it improbable that the same two men in
white are the two witnesses who shall appear during the dreadful reign
of the Antichrist: "and they shall prophesy a thousand two hundred and
three score[2] days, clothed in sackcloth" (Rev 11:3). But whoever the
messengers may have been, whether Moses and Elias, or angels in human
form, the message itself was of sufficient importance to summon them

---

1. Elias is commonly rendered Elijah in modern translations.

2. A score is 20, so three score is 60 days, totaling 1,260 days.

from heaven, and it forms one of the three great announcements—the death, the resurrection, and the return of the Lord to the earth. Nor is it possible to mistake its meaning. This same Jesus who bore the marks of the nails in His hands and of the spear wound in His side; this same Jesus who said to His disciples, "Handle me, and see; for a spirit hath not flesh and bones, as ye see me have" (Luke 24:39); this same Jesus who ate and talked with them; this same Jesus who ascended from their midst bodily, and personally and visibly, "this same Jesus, which is taken up from you into heaven, shall so come in like manner as ye have seen Him go into heaven" (Acts 1:11).

Bengel has well said, "Between His ascension and His coming in glory, no event intervenes equal in importance to each of these two events. There lore these two are joined together, and it accords with the majesty of Christ that during the whole period between His ascension and His advent He should without intermission be expected."

Rev. A. Maclaren, D. D., of Manchester, England, one of the ablest and most accomplished among living expositors, truly remarks:

> "He will 'so come in like manner as' He has gone. We are not to water down such words as these with anything short of a return precisely corresponding in its method to the departure; and as the departure was visible, corporeal, literal, personal and local, so, too, will be His return from heaven to earth. And He will come as He went, a visible manhood, only thronged, amidst the clouds of heaven, with powder and great glory. This is the aim that He sets before Him in His departure; He goes in order that He may come back again."

Hence we are not surprised to find that the prediction and promise of the two men in white became a prominent theme in the preaching of the apostles. Thus a few days after the ascension, Peter said to the people:

"Repent ye, therefore, and be converted, that your sins
may be blotted out, so that the times of refreshing shall
come from the presence of the Lord; and He shall send
Jesus Christ, which before was preached unto you: whom
the heaven must receive until the times of restitution of all
things, which God hath spoken by the mouth of all His
holy prophets since the world began" (Acts 3:19–21).

The heaven, then, must give back Jesus at the times of the restitution of
all things, and this has been the subject of divine revelation through the
prophets since the world began. It is wild exegesis which imagines that
the heaven must receive Him until the end of the times of the restitution
of all things. If a friend writes to another that he will stay where he is until
Spring, it would be foolish to fancy that he means until the end of Spring.
But the exegesis proves too much, for if Christ will not come until the
end of the times of the restitution of all things, he will not come at all,
since the times of the restitution of all things include the final judgment,
and the new heavens and new earth. It is obvious to every unprejudiced
reader that Christ comes from heaven to inaugurate and introduce these
times.

The possible nearness of this personal return from heaven is shown by
the fact that in the first epistle Paul was directed by the Holy Spirit to
write, he does not hesitate to describe the Thessalonians as those who
had "turned to God from idols, to serve the living and true God; and to
wait for His Son from heaven, whom He raised from the dead, even Jesus, which delivered us from the wrath to come" (1 Thess 1:9–10). That
this is a personal return cannot be doubted, for neither the Holy Spirit,
nor death, nor the destruction of Jerusalem, nor any other providential
event is ever called Jesus, nor were they raised from the dead, nor did they
deliver us from the wrath to come. It is certain, therefore, that believers
eighteen hundred years ago were taught by inspiration to wait for God's
Son from heaven.

Then comes another statement in the next chapter: "What is our hope,
or joy, or crown of rejoicing? Are not even ye in the presence of our

Lord Jesus Christ at His coming?" (1 Thess 2:19). Then comes another statement in the next chapter: "The Lord make you to increase and abound in love one toward another, and toward all men, even as we do toward you: to the end He may stablish your hearts unblameable in holiness before God, even our Father, at the coming of the Lord Jesus Christ with all His saints" (1 Thess 3:12–13).

Then comes another statement in the next chapter: "The Lord Himself shall descend from heaven with a shout" (1 Thess 4:16). No one pretends to make out of these passages anything except a literal and personal return of Jesus, and the ingenuity of the keenest criticism fails to discover a reference in them to any other event whatsoever.

Then comes another statement in the next chapter: "Of the times and the seasons, brethren, ye have no need that I write unto you. For yourselves know perfectly that the day of the Lord so cometh as a thief in the night" (1 Thess 5:1–2). How did the Thessalonians, who had but recently turned to God from idols, know this so perfectly? Plainly because the Apostle during his brief visit had taught it to them. It was not, then, a subject of no practical value in his estimation, as so often affirmed now, and it cannot be right to dismiss it from the field of contemplation and discussion, as preachers and people generally do at present. No matter whether he is a premillennialist or postmillennialist, every ambassador for Christ is bound to testify of the Lord's personal return from heaven; and to substitute for it the manifestation of the Spirit's power, the progress of the church, or the advance of Christian civilization, is a dangerous and deplorable departure from the truth of God. Well may we join in the apostle's prayer, "The very God of peace sanctify you wholly; and I pray God your whole spirit and soul and body be preserved blameless at the coming of our Lord Jesus Christ" (1 Thess 5:23).

Turning now to the second epistle to the Thessalonians, and the second the apostle was inspired to write, we find the same great truth prominently brought forth. Thus to the persecuted Christians it is said in the first chapter:

"To you who are troubled rest with us when the Lord
Jesus shall be revealed from heaven with His mighty angels, in flaming fire taking vengeance on them that know
not God, and that obey not the gospel of our Lord Jesus
Christ, who shall be punished with everlasting destruction from the presence of the Lord, and from the glory
of His power, when He shall come to be glorified in His
saints, and to be admired in all them that believe (because
our testimony among you was believed) in that day" (2
Thess 1:7–10).

In the second chapter he says, "Now we beseech you, brethren, by the
coming of our Lord Jesus Christ, and by our gathering together unto
Him, that ye be not soon shaken in mind, or be troubled, neither by
spirit, nor by word, nor by letter as from us, as that the day of the Lord
is at hand," or "is now present," as the Revised Version renders it; or
"hath arrived," as Dr. Young translates it; or "is come," as Alford gives
it; or "has set in," according to Rotherham. Our postmillennial brethren
tell us we are solemnly forbidden to believe that "the Lord is at hand,"
but surely they forget that the same Holy Spirit, by the same apostle,
elsewhere declares that "the Lord is at hand" (Phil 4:5). Would they make
the inspired writer contradict himself in this fashion? Dr. John Lillie in
his admirable lectures on the epistle truly says, "The phrase *is at hand*
occurs twenty times elsewhere in the New Testament, and not once does
it stand for the Greek word so rendered here. The word translated *is at
hand* occurs seven times, and is always rendered 'is present' but once."[3]
It is simply impossible that those who were taught in the first epistle to
look with delight for the coming of Christ, could be violently agitated by
the thought that he might be at hand. Their trouble arose from a rumor
that He had returned to the earth, and if this was true they knew that

---

3. The word "at hand" in 2 Thess 2:2 (ἐνίστημι) also shows up in Rom
8:38; 1 Cor 3:22; 7:26; Gal 1:4; 2 Tim 3:1 (future tense); Heb 9:9.

they had not been caught up in clouds to meet Him in the air, and hence their distress was extreme, as the Greek implies.

In the third chapter the apostle writes, "The Lord direct your hearts into the love of God, and into the patient waiting for Christ" (2 Thess 3:5), or "into the patience of Christ," who is patiently waiting the times and seasons which the Father has put under His own authority. So overshadowing is the doctrine of our Lord's second coming in the two epistles, it is not strange that the translators of our common version speak of "the patient waiting for Christ." It is the theme of every chapter, and no one pretends that the passages quoted refer to anything but His personal advent. It is impossible that any one of them was designed to teach the destruction of Jerusalem, or the descent of the Spirit, or the death of the believer.

It is surely also His personal coming that is in view when the same apostle writes to the Corinthians:

- "Ye come behind in no gift, waiting for the coming of our Lord Jesus Christ" (1 Cor 1:7).

- "Therefore judge nothing before the time, until the Lord come" (1 Cor 4:5).

- "As often as ye eat this bread, and drink this cup, ye do show the Lord's death till He come" (1 Cor 11:26).

All expositors no doubt would fully agree with Dr. Charles Hodge on the first of these passages:

"The second advent of Christ, so clearly predicted by Himself and by His apostles, connected as it is with the promise of the resurrection of His people and the consummation of His kingdom, was the object of longing expectation to all the early Christians. So great is the glory connected with that event that Paul in Romans 8:18–23, not only represents all present afflictions as trifling in

comparison, but describes the whole creation as looking
forward to it with earnest expectation (cf. Phil 3:20; Titus
2:13). So general was this expectation that Christians were
characterized as those 'who love His appearing,' (2 Tim
4:8), and as those 'who wait for Him' (Heb 9:28)."

Mr. Barnes, too, certainly expresses the views of all kinds and classes
of commentators, when he says on the same verse:

"The earnest expectation of the Lord Jesus became one
of the marks of early Christian piety. This return was
promised by the Saviour to His anxious disciples when
He was about to leave them (John 14:3). The promise
was renewed when he ascended to heaven (Acts 1:11).
It became the settled hope and expectation of Christians
that He would return (Titus 2:13; 2 Pet 3:12; Heb 9:28).
And with earnest prayer that He would quickly come,
John closes the volume of inspiration (Rev 22:20)."

Both of these eminent expositors were postmillennialists, as is Prof.
Beet who says of the words here expounded, "The Corinthians already
possessed spiritual gifts which were a proof of God's favor; while at the
same time they were eagerly looking forward to that day when Jesus will
visibly appear to bring in the final glory." Upon the next verse he remarks,
"To the clay of Christ's return the early Christians looked forward, as
Israel did ages before to the day of Jehovah."

But leaving for the present the inspired writings of Paul, it will be
found that each of the apostles dwells upon the great subject of our
Lord's personal return. Thus James says, "Be patient therefore, brethren,
unto the coming of the Lord" (James 4:7). Peter writes to his brethren,
"that the trial of your faith being much more precious than of gold that
perisheth, though it be tried with fire, might be found unto praise and
honor and glory at the appearing of Jesus Christ" (1 Pet 1:7); "looking for
and hastening the coming of the day of God," or as the Revised renders

it, "earnestly desiring the coming" (2 Pet 3:12). John says, "And now, little children, abide in Him; that, when he shall appear, we may have confidence, and not be ashamed before Him at His coming" (1 John 2:28). Jude says, "Enoch also, the seventh from Adam, prophesied of these, saying, behold the Lord cometh with ten thousands of His saints" (Jude 14). Finally, John opens the Apocalypse with the announcement, "Behold, He cometh with clouds, and every eye shall see Him, and they also which pierced Him, and all kindreds of the earth shall wail because of Him. Even so, Amen" (Rev 1:7).

Not a text thus far quoted can be forced to refer, even by the wildest license of the most audacious criticism, to any event whatever except the literal and personal return of the Lord Jesus. The thoughtless habit of skimming over such testimony with a passing impression that it may relate to death, or the destruction of Jerusalem, or the outpouring of the Spirit, or some striking providential event, is little less than trifling with the sacred Scriptures, and betokens a state of mind far from intelligent, and a condition of heart far from reverential. If Christians will ask themselves why they believe that Jesus was born, that He performed miracles and uttered the sayings ascribed to Him, that He died upon the cross and rose from the grave, they can easily see that they have precisely the same evidence, only multiplied tenfold, to convince them of His coming again.

It is the one object set before us, the "one hope of your calling" (Eph 4:4). As Graham on Ephesians, a capital book issued by the Presbyterian Board of Publication, well says on these words, all other hopes are:

> "united in the one great hope which has animated the
> church from the beginning—the hope of the coming and
> kingdom of Jesus Christ, which is therefore called, by way
> of eminence, 'that blessed hope' (Titus 2:13). I think,
> therefore, that this is the one hope of our calling, and
> includes all the others. The Jews had the coming of Christ
> in the flesh as their great national hope, and we Christians
> look for His coming in glory as the substance of things

hoped for. This is the hope of the New Testament as
distinguished from that of the Old, and the Gospels and
Epistles are full of it. It animated the early Christians in
their contendings, it is embodied in the Lord's Prayer, it is
the cry of the widowed church and the groaning creation:
Come, Lord Jesus, come quickly.... The cross and the
crown, the coming of Christ in the flesh and His coming
in glory, being the historical and the prophetical, and so
the proper food for memory and hope, are the two centres
of the divine word and the divine administration around
which all the systems of grace and providence revolve.
There is one faith in the dying Lamb, and one hope in the
coming King."

"For the vision of the Bridegroom
Waits the well-beloved Bride,
Severed only for a season
From her well-beloved's side.
For the hour when morn ascendeth
And the shadows disappear,
For the signs of heavenly glory,
She is waiting, waiting here.

For the coming of the Bridegroom,
Whom, though yet unseen, we love;
For the King of Saints, returning In His glory from above;
For the shout that shakes the prison
For the trumpet loud and clear,
For the voice of the archangel,
She is waiting, waiting here.

For the light beyond the darkness,
When the reign of sin is done;
When the storm has ceased its raging,
And the haven has been won;
For the joy beyond the sorrow,
Joy of the eternal year,
For the resurrection splendor,
She is waiting, waiting here!"

2

Our Lord's Teaching

It is worthy of notice that the chapter in which our Lord first announces His purpose to build His church also contains His first distinct promise to return to earth: "The Son of man shall come in the glory of his Father, with His angels; and then He shall reward every man according to his works" (Matt 16:27). Not even by the wildest flight of the imagination can these words be made to refer to the destruction of Jerusalem, to the descent of the Spirit on the day of Pentecost, to death, or to any, providential event whatever, because at none of these times has He come in the glory of His Father, with His angels, to reward every man according to his works. Whatever meaning, therefore, may be attached to His second coming in certain other passages, no one will pretend that in His earliest testimony upon this great subject He taught other than His literal and personal advent.

The same thing is true of His next positive teaching with regard to His second advent. The apostles, who had forsaken all to follow Him, wished to know what reward they should receive: "and Jesus said unto them, Verily I say unto you, That ye which have followed me, in the regeneration, when the Son of man shall sit in the throne of His glory, ye also shall sit upon twelve thrones judging the twelve tribes of Israel" (Matt 19:28). Surely no one will claim that this promise was fulfilled at the destruction of Jerusalem, or on the day of Pentecost, or at the death of the apostles, or at any time in the past, because the apostles have not yet sat on twelve thrones, judging the twelve tribes of Israel, nor has the regeneration, the renovation of the world, yet occurred. It looks forward to a glorious change on the earth, for the twelve tribes of Israel are found only on the earth, a change so splendid it is called the regeneration, or new birth, which occurs at "the times of restitution of all things" (Acts 3:21), when the Son of man shall sit in the throne of his glory, and associate the apostles as princes with Himself in the administration of His kingdom.

Nor can his next allusion to His coming be perverted to mean anything else than His literal and personal return. He answers the question of His disciples concerning the sign of His coming, and of the end of the age, by telling them that during the interval of His absence, "nation shall rise against nation, and kingdom against kingdom; and there shall be famines, and pestilences, and earthquakes, in divers places. All these are the beginning of sorrows" (Matt 24:7–8). There is the most striking parallel between the testimony of our Lord in His Olivet discourse and the testimony of the Spirit at the opening of the seals.

(1) "Many shall come in my name, saying, I am Christ; and shall deceive many" (Matt 24:5). "And I saw, and beheld a white horse: and he that sat on him had a bow, and a crown was given unto him [the *stephanos* of man, not the *diadems* of Christ in Rev 19:12]: and he went forth conquering and to conquer," the Antichrist (Rev 7:2).

(2) "And ye shall hear of wars, and rumors of wars: see that ye be not troubled: for all these things must come to pass, but the end is not yet" (Matt 24:6). "And there went out another horse that was red: and power was given to him that sat thereon to taken peace from the earth, and that they should kill one another: and there was given unto him a great sword" (Rev 6:4).

(3) "And there shall be famines" (Matt 24:7). "And I beheld, and lo, a black horse; and he that sat on him had a pair of balances in his hand, and I heard a voice in the midst of the four living creatures, saying, A measure of wheat for a penny, and three measures of barley for a penny" (Rev 6:6).

(4) "And pestilences and earthquakes in divers places" (Matt 24:7). Of the rider on the ghastly horse, whose name is Death, followed by Hell, it is said, "Power was given unto them over the fourth part of the earth to kill with the sword, and with hunger, and with death, and with the beasts of the earth" (Rev 6:8).

(5) "Then they shall deliver you up to be afflicted, and shall kill you" (Matt 24:9). "And when He had opened the Fifth Seal, I saw under the altar the souls of them that were slain for the word of God, and for the testimony which they held" (Rev 6:9).

(6) "Immediately after the tribulation of those days shall the sun be darkened, and the moon shall not give her light, and the stars shall fall from heaven" (Matt 24:29). "And I beheld when He had opened the Sixth Seal, and lo, there was a great earthquake; and the sun became black as sackcloth of hair, and the moon became as blood; and the stars of heaven fell unto the earth" (Rev 6:12)

(7) "And He shall send His angels with a great sound of a trumpet; and they shall gather together His elect from the four winds, from one end of heaven to the other" (Matt 24:31). "And He cried with a loud voice to the four angels, to whom it was given to hurt the earth and the sea, saying, Hurt not the earth, neither the sea, nor the trees, till we have sealed the servants of our God in their foreheads. And I heard the number of them that were sealed: and there were sealed an hundred and forty and four thousand of all the tribes of the children of Israel" (Rev 7:2–8).

Truly, "all these are the beginning of sorrows." The word for *sorrows* here means *travailing pangs*, issuing at last in the regeneration or new birth, but meanwhile going on to a "great tribulation, such as was not since the beginning of the world to this time, no, nor ever shall be" (Matt 24:21).

> "Immediately after the tribulation of those days"—not two thousand nor one thousand years after, but *immediately* after—"shall the sun be darkened, and the moon shall not give her light, and the stars shall fall from heaven, and the powders of the heavens shall be shaken, and then shall appear the sign of the Son of man in heaven; and then shall all the tribes of the earth mourn, and they shall see the Son of man coming in the clouds of heaven, with power and great glory. And He shall send His angels with a great sound of a trumpet; and they shall gather together

His elect from the four winds, from one end of heaven to
the other" (Matt 24:29–31).

Since it is certain that none of these events occurred at the destruction
of Jerusalem by Titus, nor on the day of Pentecost, nor at the death of
Christians, it is equally certain that when our Lord says all the tribes of
the earth shall see Him coming in the clouds of heaven, He refers to His
literal, personal and visible advent.

In like manner, He says, "When the Son of man shall come in His
glory, and all the holy angels with Him, then shall He sit upon the throne
of His glory: and before Him shall be gathered all nations" (Matt 25:31).
It may be objected that it is a waste of time to quote passages that are so
obvious in their bearing upon His literal coming no one disputes their
teaching for a moment. But the question is, why accept these as literal,
and put a figurative meaning upon passages that are equally explicit
in teaching His personal advent? For example, we constantly hear at
funerals, or read in funeral discourses, the admonition of our Saviour,
"Be ye therefore ready also: for the Son of man cometh at an hour when
ye think not" (Luke 12:40). Nine Christians out of ten have no thought
connected with these words beyond the necessity of readiness for death,
because they have been so instructed. But why associate them with death
any more than in other passages that, confessedly, contain no allusion to
death? The Lord is not here referring to death, even in the most distant
way, but to His personal return, which formed the most prominent
theme of His meditation and discourse. If the verses that contain allusion
to it in the four gospels are counted, it will be found that it occupied His
attention more than any other one subject; and surely we should give to
His language its natural and obvious meaning.

It would be well to remember this when we read the familiar words, "If
I go and prepare a place for you, I will come again, and receive you unto
myself; that where I am, there ye may be also" (John 14:3). In the first
place, Jesus frequently mentions his own death, and distinctly speaks of
the death of Peter; and hence if death had been the thought in His mind,
He would have mentioned it here. In the second place, it was as easy for

Him to say, "you shall die," as it was to say, "I will come again"; and hence the latter, not the former, was the subject of His promise. In the third place, it was a deception if He *said*, "I will come again," and *meant*, "you must die." If a beloved friend makes us sad by the announcement of his departure, and then cheers our sorrowful hearts with the promise, "I will come again," leaving us to discover after his departure that he took that method of informing us that we must die, we could not think well of his candor. In the fourth place, Jesus does not come again at our death, but the uniform mode of the New Testament in describing the death of the believer is to say we go to be with Him. In the fifth place, He is spiritually present with His people all the time, and hence does not come to them spiritually at death. In the sixth place, His coming after the resurrection, or on the day of Pentecost, or at the destruction of Jerusalem, did not fulfill the promise, "I will receive unto myself." In the seventh place, He nowhere else speaks of His coming as death, but the opposite of death. The Saviour was in heaven, not on earth, when Stephen died, and the martyr looked up steadfastly with the joyful cry, "Lord Jesus, receive my spirit" (Acts 8:59). "Willing rather to be absent from the body, and to be present with the Lord" (2 Cor 5:8), by going to Him, not by His coming to us. "Having a desire to depart, and to be with Christ" (Phil 1:23), not by His coming but by our departure. Peter speaks of putting off his tabernacle, and of his "exodus" out of the world (2 Pet 1:14–15),[1] but neither he nor any other New Testament writer represents death as the coming of Christ. It is strange, therefore, that a vast majority of Christians, without much thought, it is presumed, regard the promise of the Lord, "If I go, I will come," as only meaning, now that He has gone they must die. If it be said that the promise, taken literally, has not been fulfilled to the apostles, it is true. Their bodies are still waiting in hope for His Coming.

Dr. David Brown, who is accepted by the postmillennial brethren as the highest authority, quotes the promise, and then devotes five pages of

---

1. In 2 Pet 1:15, the KJV uses the word "decease" to translate the Greek word ἔξοδος (exodus).

his book to a very successful attempt at proving that it cannot refer to death except by way of analogy.

> "It can never be warrantable, and is often dangerous, to make that the primary and proper interpretation of a passage which is but a secondary, though it may be a very legitimate and even irresistible application of it.... 'Let not your heart be troubled (said Jesus to His sorrowing disciples). In my Father's house are many mansions; I go to prepare a place for you, and if I go away'—what then? 'Ye shall follow me? Death shall shortly bring us together?' Nay, but 'if I go away I will come again and receive you unto myself; that where I am, there ye may be also.' And how know we that, by putting this event out of its scriptural place in the expectations of the church, we are not, in a great degree, destroying its character and power as a practical principle? Can we not believe, though unable to trace it, that God's methods are ever the best; and that as in nature, so perhaps in revelation, a modification by us of the divine arrangements, apparently slight, and attended even with some seeming advantages, may be followed by a total and unexpected change of results, the opposite of what is anticipated and desired? So we fear it to be here."

But our Lord Himself leaves no possible room for the idle conjecture that in His frequent predictions of His coming He meant the death of Christians. He plainly told Peter "by what death he should glorify God. And when he had spoken this. He saith unto him, follow me. Then Peter, turning around, seeth the disciple whom Jesus loved following," unbidden, but following because he loved to be with Jesus. "Peter, seeing him, saith to Jesus, Lord, and what shall this man do? Jesus saith unto him, if I will that he tarry till I come, what is that to thee? Follow thou me. Then went this saying abroad among the brethren, that that disciple should not die: yet Jesus said not unto him, he shall not die; but, if I will that he tarry till I come, what is that to thee?" (John 21:19–23).

From this it is as plain as the shining of the sun that the disciples did not understand the coming of Christ and death to mean one and the same thing. They understood them to mean just the opposite of each other, believing that the coming of Christ would prevent the death of John, a conviction "into which they more easily fell," as Dr. David Brown informs us, "from the prevalent belief that Christ's second coming was then near at hand."

Owing to this saying of our Lord a rumor prevailed for a long time in the church that John had not died, and could not die; and Theophylact speaks of a tradition that he is kept alive somewhere, to be slain with Elias by the Antichrist. It is certain, therefore, that the early Christians did not regard the promise, "I will come again," as fulfilled in their death. It was not death, hateful and hideous death, He set before them as their hope, nor was it the destruction of Jerusalem, which Gerhard truly says "is never in one instance in Scripture called the coming of Christ," nor is it even the abiding presence of the Holy Spirit, sweet and comfortable as it is to know that He dwells with us and in us forever; but it was the return of the Lord Himself. Although death is a common theme of thought and discourse among Christians now, it is seldom mentioned in the New Testament, and in the passages that contain allusions to it, generally the word *sleep* is employed. "The grave is not the goal" placed before the believer, nor the repose of the disembodied state, nor happy experiences along the way, but the Saviour's advent to take body and soul home. "Never do we please Christ so much," says Dr. David Brown, "as when we 'refuse to be comforted,' even with His own consolations, save in the prospect of *His Personal Return*" (emphasis Brown's).

"Let not my eyes with tears be dim,
Let joy their upward glance illume;
Look up, and watch, and wait for Him
Soon, soon the Lord will come.

Soon will that star-paved milky way,
Soon will that beauteous azure dome,
Glories, ne'er yet conceived, display—
Soon, soon the Lord will come.

Changed in the twinkling of an eye,
Invested with immortal bloom,
I shall behold Him throned on high,
And sing, 'The Lord is come!'

One beam from His all-glorious face
These mortal garments will consume,
Each sinful blemish will efface—
Lord Jesus, quickly come!

What will it be with Thee to dwell,
Thyself my everlasting Home!
Oh, bliss—Oh, joy ineffable!
Lord Jesus, quickly come!"

3

His Coming May Be Near

All who read the New Testament carefully must perceive that our Lord, and then the Holy Ghost by the apostles, represent His second advent as possible at any time.

> "Watch, therefore; for ye know not what hour your Lord doth come. But know this, that if the goodman of the house had known in what watch the thief would come, he would have watched, and would not have suffered his house to be broken up. Therefore be ye also ready: for in such an hour as ye think not, the Son of man cometh" (Matt 24:42–44).

This sounds like His admonition to the unfaithful Church of Sardis:

> "I know thy works, that thou hast a name, that thou livest, and art dead. Be watchful, and strengthen the things which remain, that are ready to die: for I have not found thy works perfect before God. Remember therefore how thou hast received and heard; and hold fast, and repent. If therefore thou shalt not watch, I will come on thee as a thief, and thou shalt not know what hour I will come upon thee" (Rev 2:1–3).

"Take ye heed, watch and pray: for ye know not when the
time is. For the Son of man is as a man taking a far journey,
who left his house, and gave authority to his servants,
and to every man his work, and commanded the porter
to watch. Watch ye, therefore; for ye know not when the
master of the house cometh, at even, or at midnight, or at
the cockcrowing, or in the morning; lest coming suddenly,
he find you sleeping. And what I say unto you, I say unto
all, Watch" (Mark 13:33–37).

Here the word for *watch* in the first verse means "to lie awake, to
be sleepless," and in the three other places it means to "awaken, wake
up, rouse, stir," as if the Lord would say, in the evening "lie awake," at
midnight, at the cockcrowing, in the morning, "wake up." He seems to
anticipate the discoveries of modern science, for if He should descend at
this moment from heaven, and call His scattered saints to meet Him in
the air, to some it would be the evening, to others midnight, to others the
cockcrowing, and to others later in the morning. But it is obvious that
He wishes us to be on the lookout for Him every hour.

"Let your loins be girded about, and your lights burning:
and ye yourselves like unto men that await for their Lord,
when He will return from the wedding; that, when he
cometh and knocketh, they may open unto Him immediately. Blessed are those servants, whom the Lord, when He
cometh, shall find Watching: verily, I say unto you, that
He shall gird Himself, and make them to sit down to meat,
and will come forth and serve them. And if He shall come
in the second watch, or come in the third watch, and find
them so, blessed are those servants.... Be ye therefore ready
also: for the Son of man cometh at an hour when ye think
not" (Luke 12:35–40).

This is followed by a very solemn warning against the present common habit of saying that He cannot come for a thousand years, or, as some assert, for one hundred thousand years.

> "If that servant say in his heart, My Lord delayeth His coming; and shall begin to beat the men servants and maidens, and to eat and drink, and be drunken; the Lord of that servant will come in a day when he looketh not for Him, and at an hour when he is not aware, and will cut him in sunder, and will appoint him his portion with the unbelievers" (Luke 12:45–46).

The epistles also are full of the thought that the coming of Christ may be at hand.

- "Even we ourselves groan within ourselves, waiting for the adoption, the redemption of our body" (Rom 8:23), and the redemption, we know, can occur only at the second advent.

- "Waiting for the coming of our Lord Jesus Christ" (1 Cor 1:7).

- "Let your gentleness be known unto all men. The Lord is at hand" (Phil 4:5).

- "Ye turned to God from idols, to serve the living and true God; and to wait for His Son from heaven, whom He raised from the dead, Jesus, who delivered us from the wrath to come" (1 Thess 1:9–10).

- "The Lord Himself shall descend from heaven with a shout; and the dead in Christ shall rise first: then we which are alive and remain, shall be caught up together with them in clouds, to meet the Lord in the air" (1 Thess 4:16–17).

It is evident that the apostle hoped to be alive at the descent of the Lord Himself from heaven to summon His waiting ones to meet Him in the air. We are not surprised, therefore, to find him describing the proper attitude of the believer as "looking for that blessed hope and appearing of the glory of our great God and Saviour Jesus Christ" (Titus 2:13).

- "Unto them that look for Him shall He appear the second time without sin unto salvation" (Heb 9:28).

- "For yet a little while, and He that shall come will come, and will not tarry" (Heb 10:37).

- "Be ye also patient; stablish your hearts: for the coming of the Lord draweth nigh" (James 5:8).

- "The end of all things is at hand: be ye therefore sober, and watch unto prayer" (1 Pet 4:7).

Concerning 1 Peter 4:7, Calvin remarks:

> "The end he speaks of is not merely that of each individual, but the entire renovation of the world; as if he said, that Christ will shortly come, and put an end to all things.... Did the trump of Christ sound in our ears, it would keenly smite all our senses, nor suffer them to lie thus torpid. It might be objected, however, that a long series of ages has elapsed since Peter wrote this, and still the end is not yet seen. I answer, that to us time seems long for this reason, that we measure its length by the spaces of the present life, but that, could we have respect to the perpetuity of the life to come, many generations would be for us as it were a moment (2 Pet 3:8). *Moreover, it must be held as a first principle, that, ever since the appearance of Christ, there is nothing left to the faithful, but with wakeful minds to be always intent on His second advent."*

- "Little children, it is the last time; and as ye have heard that Antichrist shall come, even now are there many Antichrists; whereby we know that it is the last time" (1 John 2:18).

- "Behold, I come quickly: hold that fast which thou hast, that no man take thy crown" (Rev 3:11).

- "Behold, I come as a thief. Blessed is he that watcheth, and keepeth his garments, lest he walk naked, and they see his shame" (Rev 16:15).

- "Behold, I come quickly: blessed is he that keepeth the sayings of the prophecy of this book" (Rev 22:7).

- "Behold, I come quickly; and my reward is with me, to give every man according as his work shall be" (Rev 22:12).

- "Surely I come quickly; amen. Even so, come, Lord Jesus" (Rev 22:20).

From this it is plain to the unprejudiced reader of the Bible, that Christ, and after Him the Holy Spirit, sought to make the impression that the second advent might occur during the generation which immediately followed the death and resurrection of the Saviour. It is needless to say that no deception was intended or practiced, for apart from the fact that such a thought would be blasphemy, we must remember that Jesus Himself tells us, "Of that day and hour knoweth no man, no, not the angels which are in heaven, neither the Son, but the Father" (Mark 13:32). As Dr. Joseph Addison Alexander truly remarks, "That such a declaration should be made at all, is wonderful enough, but scarcely credible on any supposition, or in any sense, if made in reference to the date of the destruction of Jerusalem."

To this it may be added that such a declaration could not be made in any other than the gospel according to Mark, where the purpose of the Spirit is to describe the Son of God as the obedient servant; and "the servant knoweth not what his Lord doeth" (John 15:13). It is not a denial of our Lord's divine omniscience, but simply an assertion that in the economy of human redemption it was not for Him "to know the times or the seasons, which the Father hath appointed by His own authority" (Acts 1:7). Jesus knew that He will come again, and often spoke of His second advent, but it did not fall to His office as Son to determine the date of His return, and hence He could hold it up before His followers as the object of constant expectation and desire.

In the second place, we are not competent to understand what is meant by "quickly" from the heavenly standpoint of view. There is "no night there" (Rev 22:5), no revolution of the earth upon its axis, no dragging of wearisome hours, but everlasting bliss and glory in the presence of Him with whom "a thousand years as one day" pass in perfect peace (2 Pet 3:8). Hence as time is counted in the bright skies, two days have not yet gone by since Jesus ascended from the mount of Olives.

In the third place, the church is presented in the New Testament, not as detached particles of sand, but as a unit, "and every one members one of another" (Rom 12:5). When it is a question of life she is called the body of Christ, when it is a question of love she is the bride of Christ. Considered as an organism or person, the measure of the nearness which the second advent has to one member is the measure of its nearness to all the members, and the first believers are no less concerned than the last in the blessedness of His personal return. The body will not be complete, nor will the bride be perfectly built from the wounded side of the second Adam, nor will the deep slumber of the grave be broken, until He comes again.

In the fourth place, the Redeemer's second appearing is "*the* hope set before us" (Heb 6:18). It is, in the language of Dr. David Brown, "THE VERY POLE-STAR OF THE CHURCH." The object of hope to one is the object of hope to all, or the unity of the church is destroyed, and it could no longer be true that "there is one body, and one spirit, even as ye are called in one hope of your calling, one Lord, one faith, one baptism, one God and Father of all" (Eph 4:4–6). Hence it was unavoidable, from this unity, that the early Christians also should be incited to fidelity by a hope that is common to the entire church.

In the fifth place, if our Lord referred to His second coming at all, it may be said reverently that He could not have spoken of it otherwise than He did without defeating the end for which He proclaimed it to the apostles. Archbishop Trench has well remarked:

> "It is not that He desires each succeeding generation to believe that He will certainly return in their time, for He does not desire our faith and our practice to be founded on an error, as, in that case, the faith and practice of all generations except the last would be. *But it is a necessary element of the doctrine concerning the second coming of Christ, that it should be possible at any time, that no generation should consider it improbable in theirs.*"

Rev. John Ker, D. D., also says:

> "It is in the New Testament the great event that towers above every other. The heaven that gives back Christ gives back all that we have loved and lost, solves all doubts, and ends all sorrows. His coming looks in upon the whole life of the church, as a lofty mountain peak looks in upon every little valley and sequestered house around its base, and belongs to them all alike. Every generation lies under the shadow of it."

It is not strange, therefore, to find Jesus Christ and the Spirit teaching the early disciples to look for the second advent of our Lord, nor is it strange to find the apostles in their inspired writings expressing the hope that He might return in their day. The fact is that there is no predicted event between this passing moment and the coming of the Lord *for* His saints, although prophecies remain to be fulfilled between the present hour and the appearing of the Lord *with* His saints.

The first Christians were precisely right, as we are, in maintaining an attitude of constant looking for Him, without having their minds diverted by current events. On the first day of the week they met to "show the Lord's death till He come" (1 Cor 11:26). It was not revealed to them when He will come back, but it was revealed that He desired them to be in a posture of constant waiting and watching for Himself. Whether we can understand the reasonableness of His will or not, it is wise to heed His command. "Behold, to obey is better than to sacrifice, and to hearken, than the fat of rams" (1 Sam 15:22).

An order of godly monks, known as Sleepless Ones, was founded on the Bosporus in AD 430. They numbered 300, and were divided into six choirs, so that day and night their hymns ascended to our risen Lord. They sang and watched continually for the coming of the Bridegroom. But at last silence and sleep succeeded song and vigilance, and spiritual life was dwarfed in Europe for a thousand years.

> "How long, Oh Lord our Saviour,
> Wilt thou remain away?
> Some hearts are growing weary,
> For Thy so long delay.
> Oh, when shall come the moment,
> When, brighter far than morn,
> The sunlight of thy glory
> Shall on Thy people dawn?
>
> How long, Oh heavenly Bridegroom
> How long dost thou delay?
> And yet, how few are grieving,
> That Thou dost absent stay!
> Thy very bride her portion
> And calling hath forgot.
> And seeks for ease and pleasure,
> Where Thou, her Lord, art not.

Awake Thy slumbering virgins.
Send forth the solemn cry.
Let all Thy saints repeat it—
The Bridegroom draweth nigh.
Let all our lamps be burning,
Our loins well-girded be,
Each eager heart expecting
With joy Thy face to see."

4

The Present Age

The word for *age* is usually and improperly translated *world* in our authorized version. The following are examples:

- "The harvest is the end of the age" (Matt 13:39).

- "Lo, I am with you alway, even unto the end of the age" (Matt 28:20).

- "Be not conformed to this age" (Rom 12:2).

- "The god of this age hath blinded the minds of them which believe not" (2 Cor 4:4).

- Christ "gave Himself for our sins, that He might deliver us from this present evil age" (Gal 1:4).

- God "set Him at His own right hand in the heavenlies, far above all principality, and power, and might, and dominion, and every name that is named, not only in this age, but also in that which is to come" (Eph 1:20–21).

- "The rulers of the darkness of this age" (Eph 6:12).

- "Having loved this present age" (2 Tim 4:10).

- "The powers of the age to come" (Heb 6:5).

Bagster's Analytical Lexicon gives as the definition of the word, "a period of time of significant character; life, an era; an age; hence, a state of things marking an age or era; the present order of nature; the natural condition of man, the world." It stands, of course, in contrast with the age to come, and in the New Testament the present period of time has a significant character of evil, of self-denial, sorrow, suffering, trial for the people of God, until that age to come shall burst upon their gladdened view. There is not even a hint from the first of Matthew to the last of Revelation that this significant character will be changed during the entire age in which we live, or until the second advent of Christ.

- Jesus tells us that the tares and the wheat "grow together until the harvest," and as already seen, "the harvest is the end of the age" (Matt 13:30, 39).

- "He said to them all. If any man will come after me, let him deny himself, and take up his cross daily, and follow me" (Luke 9:23).

- "If the world hate you, ye know that it hated me before it hated you. If ye were of the world, the world would love his own; but because ye are not of the world, but I have chosen you out of the world, therefore the world hateth you. Remember the word that I said unto you. The servant is not greater than his Lord. If they have persecuted me, they will also persecute you; if they have kept my saying, they will keep yours also" (John 15:18–20).

- "In the world ye shall have tribulation" (John 16:33).

- "The world hath hated them, because they are not of the world, even as I am not of the world" (John 17:14).

Where is there an intimation in the teachings of our Lord that this state of things will be changed, and that His followers will become so numerous and victorious, they shall no longer bear the cross, nor feel the hard pressure of adverse circumstances?

But do the apostles cheer us with the hope of a better time during the present age? Nay, they remind us that:

- "we must through much tribulation enter into the kingdom of God" (Acts 14:22).

- we are "heirs of God, and joint-heirs with Christ; if so be that we suffer with Him, that we may be also glorified together" (Rom 8:17).

- "unto you it is given in the behalf of Christ, not only to believe on Him, but also to suffer for His sake" (Phil 1:29)

- "if we suffer, we shall also reign with Him" (2 Tim 2:12).

- "all that will live godly in Christ Jesus shall suffer persecution; but evil men and seducers shall wax worse and worse, deceiving, and being deceived" (2 Tim 3:12–13).

- "the whole world lieth in the wicked one" (1 John 5:19).

Can a line be pointed out in any of the epistles which gives promise of a day when the saints must no more through much tribulation enter into the kingdom of God, when the godly are no more to suffer persecution, when the world is no more to lie in the wicked one? It may be said that the church does not suffer persecution now—but why? Alas! because the church has been converted to the world, and the world does not persecute its own. But let the church be separate from the world, according to our Lord's command and prayer, and it would soon be seen that the offense of the cross has not ceased.

Even if it be true that the church will extend her influence, and establish institutions of learning, and uplift the race to a loftier plane of liberty and intelligence and morality by the power of Christian civilization, what sort of a millennium would it be? Out of the present population of the earth a babe is born into the world every second, nine hundred and ninety-nine times in a thousand amid the frightful agonies of the mothers; and at every swing of the pendulum, a human being dies, nine hundred and ninety-nine times in a thousand amid pain and suffering unutterable. It is estimated that 86,400 babes, little children, youth, persons in the midst of their brief existence, and in old age, have the life choked out of them every day by the ruffian hand of violence, or by some horrible malady, 32,000,000 being tortured and slaughtered every year; and no increase of the church can avert the dreadful ravages of physical disorder and mental distress. Nay, since the time Jesus was nailed to the cross, millions of His followers have been called to face death in its most horrible form, and today tens of thousands of the most saintly women are quivering in the ruffian grasp of disease, or weeping in desolated homes over the burial of all earthly joy.

Even those who argue most earnestly, that Christ took our sicknesses in the same sense in which He took our sins, and who assert most confidently that sickness may be healed in answer to faith, sicken and die like the rest, and find out that during the present age, "it is appointed unto men once to die" (Heb 9:28). It would be amusing, if it were not so sad, to see blear-eyed, cadaverous, lop-sided men and women running around the country, and talking of the blessedness of being kept by faith in perfect soundness of body. They too become bald, and gray headed, and wrinkled, and infirm, and lose their teeth, and have headaches and heartaches, and go on tottering feet to the grave, and breathe the prayer of Moses, the man of God, "Our years we pass off like a sigh. Threescore and ten are the years of our life, or, if our strength endure, they may be fourscore years; yet at their best they are toil and emptiness; for they pass swiftly, and we fly away" (Ps 90:10).

More than eighteen hundred years ago the Holy Ghost testified, "the whole creation groaneth and travaileth together in pain until now" (Rom 8:22), and it is so still. According to the report of the Signal Service Department of the Government, during the eighteen years preceding 1891, there were 2,000 cyclones or tornadoes in the United States, killing 1,826 men, women and children, and destroying property to the amount of $34,894,700, and it is admitted that many similar storms were not reported. The air is heavy with the germs of pestilence. Each continent, nay, each state, is an Aceldama,[1] a field of blood, covered with human bodies slain in battle. Crime and cruelty and vice that might shame the wild beasts, blacken all pages of the world's history. The sea roars in rebellion and wrath against the wickedness of man. The earth trembles and quakes at his audacity. The soil yields a reluctant return to his unceasing toil. The lower animals wage ferocious war with one another; and look where we may, we behold confusion, disorder and unrest, every note of nature sounding forth in the minor key, as the musicians tell us, its sad complaint.

> "Six thousand years of sorrow have wellnigh
> Fulfilled their tardy and disastrous course
> Over a sinful world; and what remains
> Of this tempestuous state of human things
> Is merely as the working of the sea
> Before a calm that rocks itself to rest.
> ... The world appears
> To toll the death-bell of its own decease,
> And by the voice of all its elements
> To preach the general doom!"

Contrast this with the time when:

- "they shall beat their swords into plowshares, and their spears into pruning-hooks; nation shall not lift up sword against nation, neither shall they learn war any more" (Isa 2:4).

- "the wolf also shall dwell with the lamb, and the leopard shall lie down with the kid; and the calf and the young lion, and the fatling together; and a little child shall lead them" (Isa 11:6).

---

1. Aceldama is an Aramaic term which means "field of blood" and comes from Acts 1:19.

- "the inhabitant shall not say, I am sick" (Isa 33:24).

- "the desert shall rejoice and blossom as the rose" (Isa 35:1).

- God shall say, "as the days of a tree are the days of my people, and mine elect shall long enjoy the work of their hands; they shall not labor in vain, nor bring forth for trouble" (Isa 65:22–23).

It is obvious that the present age is under "the rulers of the darkness of this age" (Eph 6:12).

But may not the glowing predictions, just quoted, be fulfilled in the gradual enlargement and extension of the church? Impossible, because of the reply our Lord gave to the inquiry of His apostles, "what shall be the sign of thy coming, and of the end of the age?" (Matt 24:3). He shows that the entire interval, up to the time of His coming, will be filled with wars, and rumors of wars, nation rising against nation, and kingdom against kingdom; "and there shall be famines, and pestilences, and earthquakes in divers places. All these are the beginning of travailing pangs," which grow more and more severe, until *immediately* after an unparalleled tribulation, "such as was not since the beginning of the world," they shall see the Son of Man coming in the clouds of heaven, with power and great glory (Matt 24:4–30).

Impossible again, because the Holy Ghost, in correcting the error of the Thessalonians who feared that the day of the Lord had already come, distinctly says:

> "It will not be, except the falling away come first, and the man of sin be revealed, the son of perdition, he that opposeth and exalteth himself against all that is called God or that is worshipped; so that he sitteth in the temple of God, setting himself forth as God. Remember ye not that when I was yet with yon, I told you these things? And now ye know that which restraineth, to the end that he may be revealed in his own season? For the mystery of lawlessness doth already work; only there is one that restraineth now,

until he be taken out of the way. And then shall be revealed
the lawless one, whom the Lord Jesus shall slay with the
breath of his mouth, and bring to naught by the manifestation of His coming [or 'presence,' as the word is always
rendered when it refers to a person]" (2 Thess 2:3–8).

The mystery of lawlessness was working in Paul's day, only there was
some power hindering or restraining its outward display. But when that
hindering or restraining power, whatever it may be, is taken out of the
way, what then? Shall the church enter upon its career of peace and puri-
ty and prosperity, and the gospel lead the nations to bow to its beneficent
sway? Nay, there shall be revealed the lawless one, who is to be destroyed
by the appearing, as the word is always rendered elsewhere, of our Lord's
personal presence. It is evident, therefore, that between the departure
and return of Christ there is no place for a spiritual millennium, or for
the universal reign of righteousness.

> "Thou who from Olive's brow did'st rise
> In glorious triumph to the skies,
> Before the rapt disciples' eyes—
> Lord Jesus, quickly come!
> For Thy appearance all things pray,
> All nature sighs at Thy delay,
> Thy people cry, no longer stay.
> Lord Jesus, quickly come!
>
> Hear Thou the whole creation's groan,
> The burdened creatures' plaintive moan,
> The cry of deserts wild and lone—
> Lord Jesus, quickly come!
> See signals of distress unfurled,
> By states on stormy billows hurled,
> Thou Pole-star of a shipwrecked world.
> Lord Jesus, quickly come!

Hush the fierce blast of war's alarms.
The tocsin's toll, the clash of arms.
Incarnate Love, exert Thy charms.
Lord Jesus, quickly come!
Walk once again upon the face
Of this sad earth's tempestuous seas,
And still the waves, O Prince of Peace,
Lord Jesus, quickly come!

Lo, Thy fair Bride, with garments torn,
Of her celestial radiance shorn,
Upturns her face with watching worn—
Lord Jesus quickly come!
Her trickling tears, her piteous cries,
Her struggles, fears and agonies
Appeal to Thy deep sympathies—
Lord Jesus, quickly come!

Come, with Thy beauteous diadem,
Come, with embattled Cherubim,
Come, with the shout of Seraphim,
Lord Jesus, quickly come!
Come, on Thy seat of radiant cloud,
Come, with the Archangel's trumpet loud,
Come, Saviour, let the heavens be bowed.
Lord Jesus, quickly come!"

5

The End of the Age

If righteousness is to prevail during the present age, or before the coming of Christ, it is remarkable that He said nothing about it in the long Olivet discourse, containing 97 verses (Matt 24–25). On the other hand, He plainly says:

> "Then shall many stumble, and shall betray one another, and shall hate one another. And many false prophets shall rise, and shall deceive many. And because iniquity shall abound, the love of many shall wax cold. But he that shall endure unto the end, the same shall be saved. And this gospel of the kingdom shall be preached in all the world for a witness unto all nations; and then shall the end come" (Matt 24:10–14).

There is not a line in the New Testament which shows that the gospel is to be preached for the conversion of all nations. Although a large ecclesiastical body recently cheered at a mocking of the doctrine that it is to be proclaimed in all the world for a witness unto all nations, it was a mocking of the words of our Lord.

So far as it is from being true that light breaks in amid the stumbling, the betrayal of one another, the mutual hatred, the rise of false prophets, the deception of many, the abounding of iniquity, the waxing cold of love, things go from bad to worse until "there shall be great tribulation, such as was, not since the beginning of the world to this time, nor ever shall be." What then? A period of great spiritual power and progress and prosperity?

> "IMMEDIATELY after the tribulation of those days shall the sun be darkened, and the moon shall not give her light, and the stars shall fall from heaven, and the powers of the heavens shall be shaken; and then shall appear the sign of the Son of Man in heaven; and then shall all the tribes of the earth mourn, and they shall see the Son of Man coming in the clouds of heaven with power and great glory. And He shall send His angels with a great sound of a trumpet, and they shall gather together His elect from the four winds, from one end of heaven to the other" (Matt 24:29–31).

The word translated *immediately* is so rendered thirty-three times, *straightway* thirty-two times, and *forthwith* seven times. The end of the age shall be reached, therefore, through terrible judgments, not through the triumphs of the church.

> "As the days of Noe were, so shall also the coming of the Son of Man be. For as in the days that were before the flood, they were eating and drinking, marrying and giving in marriage, until the day that Noe entered into the ark, and knew not until the flood came, and took them all away; so shall also the coming of the Son of Man be. Then shall two be in the field; the one shall be taken, and the other left. Two women shall be grinding at the mill; the one shall be taken, and the other left. Watch therefore: for ye know not what hour your Lord doth come" (Matt 24:37–42).

The one shall be taken to live forever with the Lord, and the other left to judgment.

"There shall come a night of such wild affright,
As none beside shall know;
When the heaven shall shake, and the wide earth quake
In its last and deepest woe.

What horrors shall roll over the godless soul,
Waked from its death-like sleep;
Of all hope bereft, and to Judgment left,
Forever to wail and weep.

O worldling, give ear, while the saints are near!
Soon must the tie be riven;
And men, side by side, God's hand shall divide;
As far as hell's depths from heaven.

Some husband, whose head was laid on his bed,
Throbbing with mad excess,
Awakes from that dream, by the lightning' gleam,
Alone in his last distress.

For the patient wife, who through each day's life
Watched and wept for his soul,
Is taken away and no more shall pray—
For the judgment thunders roll.

The children of day are summoned away;
Left are the children of night—
Sealed is their doom, for there's no more room;
Filled are the mansions of light."

"Then,"—emphatic, as Dean Alford says, "viz, the coming of the Lord to His personal reign"—"Then shall the kingdom of heaven be likened unto ten virgins, which took their lamps, and went forth to meet the bridegroom." Dr. David Brown says, "*Then*—at the time referred to at the close of the preceding chapter, the time of the Lord's Second Coming to reward His faithful servants and to take vengeance on the faithless;" and "so essential a feature of the Christian character, according to the New Testament, is looking for Christ's Second Appearing, that both real and apparent disciples are here described as going forth to meet Him."

No doubt all expositors and Christians agree that the ten virgins represent the professed followers of Christ (Matt 25:1–13). Hence it is important to notice that "while the Bridegroom tarried they all nodded and slept." It is only when the midnight cry is heard, "Behold the Bridegroom cometh," they awake. The end, therefore will not find the professing church watching and working.

On another occasion our Lord said:

> "As it was in the days of Noe, so shall it be also in the days
> of the Son of Man. They did eat, they drank, they married
> wives, they were given in marriage, until the day Noe
> entered into the ark, and the flood came, and destroyed
> them all. Likewise also as it was in the days of Lot; they did
> eat, they drank, they bought, they sold, they planted, they
> builded; but the same day that Lot went out of Sodom,
> it rained fire and brimstone from heaven, and destroyed
> them all. Even thus shall it be in the day when the Son of
> Man is revealed" (Luke 17:26–30).

There is no harm, in itself considered, in that which the people at large are represented as doing, nothing inconsistent with culture, the advance of art, the march of civilization, or the accumulation of wealth. But there may be utter ungodliness. Look at Berlin, Paris and all the cities of Christendom. "Nevertheless, when the Son of Man cometh, shall He find faith on the earth?" Of course He will find faith on the earth, when

He calls His waiting ones to meet Him in the air; but when He comes with them, "shall He find faith on the earth?" (Luke 18:8).

It is the popular belief, even in the church, that the world is moving on to a splendid future, and that knowledge, freedom and social order will mark the close of the present age. But Jesus says that at the winding up there shall be "upon the earth distress of nations, with perplexity; the sea and the waves roaring; men's hearts failing them for fear, and for looking after those things which are coming on the earth; for the powers of heaven shall be shaken. And then shall they see the Son of Man coming in a cloud with power and great glory" (Luke 21:25–27). Hence He adds the admonition:

> "Take heed to yourselves, lest at any time your hearts be overcharged with surfeiting,[1] and drunkenness, and cares of this life, and so that day come upon you unawares. For as a snare [like that which catches the unwary bird] shall it come on all them that dwell [sitting, settled down] on the face of the whole earth. Watch ye therefore, and pray always, that ye may be accounted worthy to escape all these things that shall come to pass, and to stand before the Son of Man" (Luke 21:34–36).

What He said in the same connection about Jerusalem being trodden down of the Gentiles, has been literally fulfilled, despite the efforts of Julian the Apostate, and of the Crusaders. Why should not His prediction concerning the condition of the world at the second advent be also literally fulfilled? It would be an insult to the understanding of the reader to suppose that our Lord here refers to anything but His personal coming at the end of the age.

It is needless to say that there is nothing in the epistles to contradict this plain testimony.

---

1. Surfeiting is an overindulgence in something.

"This know also, that in the last days perilous [or difficult] times shall come. For men shall be lovers of their own selves, covetous, boasters, proud, blasphemers, disobedient to parents, unthankful, unholy, without natural affection, truce-breakers, false accusers, incontinent, fierce, despisers of those that are good, traitors, heady, high-minded, lovers of pleasure more than lovers of God; having a form of godliness, but denying the power thereof" (2 Tim 3:1–5).

If such will be the condition of those who profess godliness, what must be the state of those who make no profession? Remember that this is the Holy Spirit's description of the last days. "Knowing this first," for it is important to know it, "that there shall come in the last days scoffers, walking after their own lusts, and saying, where is the promise of His coming? for since the fathers fell asleep, all things continue as they were from the beginning of the creation" (2 Pet 3:3–4). The argument of the scoffers is based upon the stability of nature's laws; and it is a suggestive fact that in our own day more and more is nature, an inanimate and unconscious thing, pushed to the foreground, and more and more is God pushed to the background, of man's contemplations. "As the lightning cometh out of the east, and shineth even unto the west; so shall also the coming of the Son of Man be" (Matt 24:27); and when that lightning's flash is seen, causing the solid pillars of the globe to shake and tremble, the scoffs of the scientists shall suddenly be changed into shrieks of terror; but this shall be in the last days.

"Though not quite a millenarian," wrote Dr. James W. Alexander of New York, "I was struck with these words of Chalmers to Bickersteth: 'Without slacking in the least our obligation to keep forward this great [missionary] cause, I look for its conclusive establishment through a widening passage of desolating judgments, with the utter demolition of our present civil and ecclesiastical structures.'"

Just as the Holy Ghost testifies of Israel, "the end thereof shall be with a flood, and unto the end of the war desolations are determined," or as it is in the margin, "it shall be cut off by desolations" (Dan 9:26), even so the same Spirit witnesses to the ruin of Christendom: "Behold therefore the goodness and severity of God; on them which fell, severity; but toward thee, goodness, if thou continue in His goodness; otherwise thou shalt be cut off" (Rom 11:22). That the professing church has not continued in the goodness of God, alas! the most cursory glance will show, and hence she is to be set aside as Israel was, and disowned for her unfaithfulness.

"Yet once again Thy sign shall be upon the heavens displayed,
And earth and its inhabitants be horribly afraid;
For not in weakness clad, Thou com'st, our woes, our sins, to bear,
But girt with all Thy Father's might, His vengeance to declare.

The terrors of that awful day.
Oh, who can understand?
Or who abide when Thou in wrath shall lift Thy holy hand?
The earth shall quake, the sea shall roar, the sun in heaven grow pale;
But Thou hast sworn, and wilt not change, Thy faithful shall not fail.

Then grant us, Saviour, so to pass our time in watching here,
That when upon the clouds of heaven Thy glory shall appear,
Uplifting high our joyful heads, in triumph we may rise,
And enter, with Thine angel train, Thy palace in the skies."

6

Parables of Matthew 13

Our postmillennial brethren very properly insist that these parables were designed to set forth the state of things during the present age, or up to the time of Christ's second advent. This is shown by the fact that they tell us the parable of the mustard seed exhibits the growth of the church from a small beginning, "the least of all seeds," into its branching glories that will in due time afford shade and shelter for all the nations of the earth. They also inform us that the parable of the leaven indicates the spread of the gospel or of Christianity until the whole world shall be permeated with the benign influences of religion, as it is called.

But surely they will admit that no interpretation of the two parables, which the Saviour did not explain, can be correct, if forced to teach a doctrine directly opposed to the two that He did expound. Thus He announces in the parable of the sower that "the seed is the word of God." One part falls upon the hard, beaten pathway skirting the field, "and the fowls came and devoured them up," "the wicked one" (Matt 13:19), "Satan" (Mark 4:15), "the devil" (Luke 8:12). Another part falls on a thin layer of soil covering a rock, and being quickly heated the seed springs up immediately, but having no depth of root, it as soon withers.

Another part falls among thorns, and the thorns spring up, and choke the seed. Another part falls into good ground, but brings forth variously, some a hundred fold, some sixty fold, some thirty fold. Thus does our Lord describe the different effects of scattering the word of God, and where is the intimation that the time is coming when all the seed, or the larger portion of it, will find good soil and bring forth an abundant harvest? But if the parable of the mustard seed and of the leaven denotes the outward and inward expansion of the church and Christianity until universal supremacy is attained, it is obvious that their meaning is in flat contradiction of the testimony given in the parable of the sower. But history for 1,850 years confirms the truth of the Lord's statement and gives no support to the other view. Only a small part of the seed sown has become fruitful. There has been no country, no county, no city, no community, all of whose inhabitants have received Christ as their Saviour; and today not a fourth even of those who belong to any denomination or particular congregation give the slightest evidence of possessing real spiritual life. Not a fourth can be found to attend regularly the services of God's house, to be present at the prayer meeting, to teach in the Sunday school, to be separate from the world, to speak a word for Christ, really to live.

The second parable our Lord explained is that of the tares and wheat. "The kingdom of heaven is likened unto a man which sowed good seed in his field; but while men slept, his enemy came and sowed tares among the wheat" (Matt 13:24–25), the tares being a bastard wheat, so like the true that they cannot be distinguished from the latter except by their emptiness. "He that soweth the good seed is the Son of Man; the field is the world; the good seed are the children of the kingdom, but the tares are the children of the wicked one; the enemy that sowed them is the devil; the harvest is the end of the age; and the reapers are the angels" (Matt 13:37–39).

Dr. David Brown declares that the design of the parable was "to set forth the *mixed* character of the visible church till Christ come. All are agreed in this. But the millennium is as *truly*, though not in the same *degree*, a mixed state of the visible church as this is.... The millennium differs in nothing worthy of mention in the parable from the present state of the church" (emphasis Brown's).

But how does this comport with the theory that the leaven is the symbol of the gospel or of Christianity, which must work its way "till the whole was leavened"? How does it agree with the testimony of the Holy Ghost, celebrating the reign of the coming King?

- "In His days shall the righteous nourish; and abundance of peace so long as the moon endureth" (Ps 72:7).

- "They shall not hurt nor destroy in all my holy mountain; for the earth shall be full of the knowledge of the Lord, as the waters cover the sea" (Isa 11:9).

- "Thy people also shall be all righteous" (Isa 60:21).

- "They shall teach no more every man his neighbor, and every man his brother, saying, know the Lord; for they shall all know me, from the least of them unto the greatest of them, saith the Lord" (Jer 31:34).

- "For from the rising of the sun even unto the going down of the same, my name shall be great among the Gentiles; and in every place incense shall be offered unto my name, and a pure offering; for my name shall be great among the heathen, saith the Lord of hosts" (Mal 1:11).

How this state of things can be made to harmonize with the present state of things, does not appear clear to the ordinary reader; and if the millennium differs in nothing worthy of mention from the present state of the church, the Lord have mercy on us, and bring the millennium to a speedy end.

Jesus likens the growth of the church to a mustard seed that shoots up and widens out, and "when it is grown, it is the greatest among herbs, and becometh a tree, so that the birds of the air come and lodge in the branches thereof" (Matt 13:32). The word for *birds* is the same that is translated *fowls* in the parable of the sower; and inasmuch as He explains the meaning of the word in one parable, and does not explain it in the other, it is singular exegesis which supposes that He means by the second use of the word in the same discourse, something entirely unlike, and even opposed to, the meaning He gives to it in His first use of the word. If the fowls or the birds represent the wicked one, Satan, the devil, in one place, they represent the same in the other place; and the Saviour teaches that "the prince of the power of the air" will find lodgment in the branches of the great tree.

As to the parable of the leaven (Matt 13:33), it is strange that our Lord made use of sour dough, or incipient putrefaction, as a symbol of the gospel and Christianity. It is still stranger that He used as a symbol of good that which He Himself, and the apostles, and all the writers of the Bible, without a single exception, employ as the symbol of evil. Dr. Joseph Addison Alexander says, "the usage is indeed so uniform and easily accounted for from rational considerations, that nothing can outweigh it but the equally uniform judgment of interpreters and readers in all ages that this is an exception to the general rule, and that leaven, in this one place and its parallel (Luke 13:21), denotes the spreading or diffusive quality of truth and the true religion." It is not correct to say that such has been the uniform judgment of interpreters and readers in all ages. But even if it were, whether the uniform judgment of ignorant interpreters and mistaken readers should outweigh the uniform testimony of the Holy Ghost, each must decide for himself.

The leaven represents what it always represents in Scripture, that which is evil in doctrine or practice, insidiously working its way, until the whole professing mass is leavened, and the Son of God in righteous judgment exclaims, "I will spue thee out of my mouth" (Rev 3:16). Leaven first appears in connection with Sodom, and then in Egypt, and it was rigidly excluded from the houses of the Israelites during the feast that followed the Passover, two different words being employed to denote inherent evil and that which is evil in outward life (cf. Exod 12:15). It was also forbidden in any offering to the Lord, that set forth Christ (cf. Lev 2:11). It was allowed in the offerings presented at Pentecost (Lev 23:17), the admitted type of the gathering of the church, because evil was there, as we well know (cf. Acts 5:1–10). Our Lord said to His disciples, "Take heed, and beware of the leaven of the Pharisees and of the Sadducees" (Matt 16:6), "and of the leaven of Herod" (Mark 8:15). The Pharisees were the ancient legalists; the Sadducees were the ancient rationalists; the Herodians were the ancient time-servers, determined to keep in with both parties, God and the devil, Christ and the world. Into these three sects nearly the whole of the professing church may now be divided, for

the woman has succeeded well in hiding the leaven in the meal. The Holy
Ghost, writing to the Corinthians about evil practice, says, "Know ye
not that a little leaven leaveneth the whole lump?" (1 Cor 5:6). The Holy
Ghost, writing to the Galatians about evil doctrine, says, "A little leaven
leaveneth the whole lump" (Gal 5:9).

If the objection is raised that Christ would not liken the kingdom of
heaven to that which is evil, it is sufficient to reply that He likens the
kingdom to that which includes both tares and wheat (Matt 13:24–30),
which encloses both good and bad fish (Matt 13:47–50), which extends
over a wicked servant (Matt 18:23–32), which admits into it a man
who had not on a wedding garment and who was lost (Matt 22:1–13).
The phrase which occurs thirty-two times in the gospel of Matthew,[1]
and only there, does not mean heaven, nor even the church, although
there is enough of evil in the latter to justify the use of any term that
would express its rottenness, but it signifies the rule of Christ from the
heavens over that sphere in which He specially manifests His grace. The
kingdom, meanwhile, exists in mystery, or concealment, or it is not yet
made manifest; and the seven parables were spoken to show the state
of things, during the time of the mysteries of the kingdom, or "till He
come."

Having uttered four of the parables in the presence of "great multitudes," He went into a house. And when the disciples came to Him,
and He had expounded unto them the parable of the tares, which must
have been a sore discouragement of their faith and a sad clouding of their
hope, He cheered their hearts with a brighter view. After all the wretched
failure of man, He has treasure hid in a field, which is the world, and
for the sake of the treasure He buys the field, so that He will yet make
good to Israel, now scattered and hid in the world. His promise long since
forfeited, "Ye shall be a peculiar treasure unto me above all people, for all
the earth is mine" (Exod 19:5). Nay, there is something more precious
to Him still, even "one pearl of great price," His blood-bought and true

---

1. The phrase "kingdom of heaven," occurs 33 times within 32 verses
of Matthew's gospel in the KJV.

church, for which He sold all that He had, that He might wear it as a jewel on His heart forever.

Once more, the kingdom of heaven is likened unto a dragnet cast into the sea, the entire circle of the agencies and means now employed in gathering men into a profession of Christ's name. But a net does not catch all the fish in the sea, and even of those caught, some are described as good and some as bad. Hence there is to be a judgment of those professing Christianity, and a casting away of the bad, at the coming of Christ. Until that time, however, the two continue together. There is positively not a hint in the seven prophetic parables of the conversion of the world, but rather only partial success, and a mixed state, growing worse and worse to the end of the age. Is it better to consult our own views as to the future, or to submit to the testimony of God's word?

> Saviour, come! Thy friends are waiting,
> Waiting for the final day;
> Thence the promised glory dating;
> Come and bear Thy saints away.
> Come, Lord Jesus,
> Thus Thy waiting people pray.
>
> Base the wish, and vain th' endeavour,
> While on earth to find our rest;
> Till we see Thy face, we never
> Shall or can be fully blest.
> In Thy presence
> Nothing shall our peace molest.
>
> Lord, we wait for Thine appearing;
> Tarry not, Thy people say;
> Bright the prospect is, and cheering,
> Of beholding Thee that day;
> When our sorrows
> Shall for ever pass away.

Till it comes, O keep us steady,
Keep us walking in Thy ways;
At Thy call may we be ready,
And our heads with triumph raise.
Then with angels
Sing Thine everlasting praise.

7

Antichrist

The Scriptures frequently refer to the appearing in the last days of a person, or succession of persons, or a system, known as the Antichrist. Thus the Spirit writes by the Apostle John: "Little children, it is the last time, and as ye have heard that the Antichrist shall come, even now are there many antichrists; whereby we know that it is the last time" (1 John 2:18). Again, "Every spirit that confesseth not that Jesus Christ is come in the flesh is not of God; and this is that spirit of the Antichrist, whereof ye have heard that it should come; and even now already is it in the world" (1 John 4:3). Again, "Many deceivers are entered into the world, even they that confess not that Jesus Christ cometh [*coming*, present participle] in the flesh. This is the deceiver and the Antichrist" (2 John 7, Revised Version).

The early church, perhaps without an exception, believed that the predicted Antichrist is to be a person, the embodiment of human blasphemy and wickedness. The learned Greswell says:

> "The fathers are likewise agreed in considering Antichrist himself to be a real person; and no merely figurative or symbolical character. Whatever he may be, and whatever the part which he is destined to act, it was the unanimous persuasion of the elders of the church that he will be a literal character, and his part will be the part of a literal bodily agent."

Jerome, for example, writes in his commentary on Daniel 7:

> "Therefore let us say, what all the ecclesiastical writers have handed down, that, in the consummation of the world, when the kingdom of the Romans is to be destroyed, there shall be ten kings who will divide the Roman world between them: and that an eleventh will arise—a little king, etc. Let us not suppose him to be, according to the opinion of some, either Devil or Demon, but one of the human race, in whom the whole of Satan shall dwell bodily; ... for he is 'the Man of Sin,' 'the Son of perdition,' so that he dares to sit in the Temple of God, making Himself out God."

Since the Reformation, the great majority of Protestant expositors regard the prophecy concerning him as fulfilled in the character and career of the Popes and Popery. The arguments in favor of the latter view are ingenious and plausible, but if the question is submitted to the decision of the inspired writings, it will be difficult for an unprejudiced mind, searching after truth, to avoid the conclusion that the Christians nearest the apostles were correct in their opinion.

In the first place, it is written, "Who is a liar, but he that denieth that Jesus is the Christ? He is the Antichrist that denieth the Father and the Son" (1 John 2:22). Can it be truthfully said of Popery, even in its worst days, that it denieth the Father and the Son? Has it not always maintained in its councils, creeds, symbols of faith and worship that there are three persons in the Godhead? Whatever may have been its departures from the Bible in other respects, in The Canons and Decrees of the Council of Trent, it was made obligatory upon every Roman Catholic to say:

> "I believe in one God, the Father Almighty, Maker of heaven and earth, of whom are all things visible and invisible; and in one Lord Jesus Christ, the only begotten Son of God, and born of the Father before all ages: God of God,

light of light, true God of true God; begotten, not made, consubstantial with the Father, by whom all things were made; ... and in the Holy Ghost, the Lord and the giver of life, who proceedeth from the Father and the Son."

The Roman church has never wavered in its adherence to this creed, and how can it be said that it denies the Father and the Son?

In the second place, all Protestant commentators insist that Popery is described under the figure of a woman "arrayed in purple and scarlet color, and decked with gold and precious stones and pearls, having a golden cup in her hand full of abominations and filthiness of her fornications" (Rev 17:4). But this woman, "the mother of harlots," is represented as riding upon a beast which has seven heads and ten horns, universally admitted to be the Antichrist. "And the ten horns which thou sawest upon the beast, these shall hate the whore, and shall make her desolate and naked, and shall eat her flesh, and burn her with fire" (Rev 17:16). If the mother of harlots is Popery, it is impossible that the beast, which is conceded to be the Antichrist, that hates and destroys the whore, should also be Popery.

In the third place, the Holy Ghost by the Apostle Paul tells us that before the day of the Lord sets in, "there comes the apostasy first, and that man of sin shall be revealed, the son of perdition; who opposeth and exalteth himself above all that is called God, or that is worshipped; so that he, as God, sitteth in the temple of God, showing himself that he is God" (2 Thess 2:4). The temple of God is an expression applied in the Bible to but three things: the temple in Jerusalem, the church, or the body of the believer (cf. 1 Cor 3:17; 6:19). If the Pope or Popery is meant by the man of sin, the son of perdition, the Antichrist, then the Pope must be sitting in the church of God, and Popery must be the Christian church, a conclusion against which those who hold this view would be the first to protest with vehement earnestness. Besides, it is not true that the Pope has exalted himself above all that is called God, or that is worshipped. However false and impious his claims, he sends forth his decrees and proclamations as the vicegerent of God, as the vicar of

Christ, always recognizing his subordination to a power higher than his own. Of the Lawless one, or Antichrist, it is said:

> "whose coming [whose *parousia*, the same word that is used to describe our Lord's personal return] is after the working of Satan, with all power, and signs, and lying wonders, and with all deceivableness of unrighteousness in them that perish; because they received not the love of the truth, that they might be saved. And for this cause God shall send them a strong delusion, that they should believe a lie: that they all might be damned who believed not the truth, but had pleasure in unrighteousness" (2 Thess 2:9–12).

All that is in Popery or Protestantism, which accepts not the truth, or the word of God, leads on to the Antichrist; but we should distinguish between the cause and the effect, and expect at the end a personal embodiment of Satan, with Satan's power to work miracles. It will be observed that the man of sin, the son of perdition, exalts himself above all that is called God, or that is worshipped, and surely this cannot be said of a system or of a succession of persons. Nor is he a worshipper, as Popes and Popery are, but worshipped, reminding us of the words addressed to him by the Holy Ghost of old:

> "How art thou fallen from heaven, O Lucifer [Daystar, a title stolen from Christ], son of the morning! For thou hast said in thine heart, I will ascend into heaven, I will exalt my throne above the stars of God: I will sit also upon the mount of the congregation, in the sides of the north [Ps 48:2]: I will ascend above the heights of the clouds: I will be like the Most High" (Isa 14:12–14).

Bishop Horsley has well described him as:

> "that son of perdition, who shall be neither a Protestant
> nor a Papist, neither Christian, nor Jew, nor Heathen;
> who shall worship neither God, Angel, nor Saint; who will
> neither supplicate the invisible majesty of Heaven, nor fall
> down before an idol. He will magnify HIMSELF against
> everything that is called God, or is worshipped: and with
> a bold flight of impiety, soaring far above his precursors
> and types in the time of Paganism—the Sennacheribs,
> the Nebuchadnezzars, the Antiochuses, and the Heathen
> Emperors, will claim divine honors to himself exclusively,
> and consecrate an image of himself."

In the fourth place, "All the world wondered after the beast [the Antichrist], and they worshipped the dragon [the devil], which gave power unto a beast" (Rev 13:3–4). The Pope and Popery may worship the Virgin and saints, but it is not true that they worship the devil, as men are openly beginning to do in France, and Italy, and other atheistic communities. "All that dwell upon the earth shall worship him, whose names are not written in the book of life of the Lamb slain from the foundation of the world" (Rev 13:4–8). That is to say, if the Pope or Popery is the Antichrist, the hosts of Antichrist are found wholly among those who worship the Pope; and the unavoidable result stares us in the face that all who do not worship him have their names in the Lamb's book of life, including such names as Voltaire, Thomas Paine, John Stuart Mill, Darwin, Huxley, Herbert Spencer, John Morley, Bradlaugh, Ingersoll and other arrogant blasphemers. To such absurdities are men led when their minds are preoccupied with a theory which they are determined to maintain.

In the fifth place:

> "If any man worship the beast and his image, and receive
> his mark in his forehead, or in his hand, the same shall

drink of the wine of the wrath of God, which is poured
out without measure into the cup of His indignation; and
he shall be tormented with fire and brimstone in the presence of the holy angels, and in the presence of the Lamb;
and the smoke of their torment ascendeth up forever and
ever; and they have no rest day nor night, who worship the
beast and his image, and whosoever receiveth the mark of
his name" (Rev 14:9–11).

Hence if the Pope or Popery is the Antichrist, not only all who worship
the Roman Catholic Church, but all who in anywise recognize its authority, are doomed to a frightful and everlasting punishment, although
it will scarcely be denied that there have been, and are still, numbers of
really godly men and women in that communion, notwithstanding the
monstrous errors of the system.

In the sixth place, those who see nothing but the Pope or Popery in
the Antichrist are compelled to put loose and fanciful interpretations
upon the Scriptures, thus creating and fostering the wretched habit of
reading the word of God as if it does not mean what it says. In the plainest
and most explicit manner it is repeatedly stated that the duration of the
Antichrist's dreadful power is limited to "1260 days," or "forty and two
months," or "a time, times, and the dividing of time," commencing his
persecutions in the midst of the last heptad (cf. Dan 9:27), and contin-
uing them for three and one-half years. But in order to make them fit the
Roman Catholic Church, these days, so carefully defined and guarded,
are stretched out into years, whose beginning and end are subjects of the
wildest conjecture.

In the seventh place, the Antichrist shall suddenly be destroyed "in
the latter days." A stone not in hands falls upon the ten confederated
kingdoms of which he is the head, and grinds them to powder, and makes
them as the chaff of the summer threshing floors (Dan 2:28–45). "He
shall plant the tabernacles of his palace between the seas [the Dead Sea
and the Mediterranean] in the glorious holy mountain [Mount Zion];
yet he shall come to his end, and none shall help him" (Dan 11:45).

Immediately after the tribulation, which occurs under his reign, Christ appears for his overthrow (Matt 24:29–31). "Then shall be revealed the Lawless one, whom the Lord Jesus shall consume with the breath of his mouth, and destroy by the epiphany of his presence" (2 Thess 2:8). At the descent of Christ from heaven, the Antichrist and his false prophet are "cast alive into a lake of fire burning with brimstone" (Rev 19:20). All of this is utterly inconsistent with the idea of a gradual extinction, or even a violent ending, of a system or succession of persons.

Indeed the personality of the Antichrist is so distinctly and variously marked that no other thought could have ever been entertained, if it had not been for the dream that we are to find him in the Pope or Popery. Irenaeus, AD 180; Tertullian, AD 200; Hippolytus, AD 220; Origen, AD 225; Lactantius, AD 300; Athanasius, AD 340; Hilary, AD 350; Cyril of Jerusalem, AD 360; Ambrose, AD 370; Jerome, AD 390; Chrysostom, AD 400, and many others of the so-called fathers speak of him as a person, an incarnate devil, sitting in the rebuilt temple at Jerusalem when the Lord shall appear.

In "The Teaching of the Apostles," a most valuable manuscript,[1] reaching back to AD 80 or 90, it is said, "for as lawlessness increaseth they shall hate one another and persecute and betray, and then shall appear the deceiver of the world as a Son of God, and shall do signs and wonders and the earth shall be given over into his hands and he shall commit iniquities which have never been since the world began" (*Didache* 16:4). Bad as Popery is, and frightful as its persecution of God's saints in the past has been, something worse awaits an infidel world. Popery is an Antichrist, and much of Protestantism also, for it must be remembered that if she is "the mother of harlots," she has daughters, but she is not the Antichrist.

Hippolytus tells us that "the ten states, meaning the ten toes of Daniel's image, which will at length appear, will be Democracies;" and Irenaeus declares that "the adversary will sit in a temple built in Jerusalem, endeavoring to show himself to be Christ." He is a counterfeit Christ, and Greswell endeavors to prove that his title means *another*

---

1. This source is also commonly referred to as The Didache.

Christ, a *pro* Christ, a *vice*-Christ. But the contrasts between the believer's Christ and the world's Antichrist are very great and striking.

- The former came down from heaven (John 6:38); the latter ascends out of the abyss (Rev 11:7).

- The former came in His Father's name (John 5:43); the latter comes in his own name.

- The former humbled Himself (Phil 2:8); the latter exalts himself (2 Thess 2:4).

- The former was despised and rejected of men (Isa 53:3); the latter has all the world saying, "Who is like the beast?" (Rev 13:3–4).

- The former received a commandment from the Father what he should say, and what he should speak (John 12:49); the latter will receive his power, and his seat, and his great authority from the devil (Rev 13:4).

- The former came to do His Father's will (John 5:30); the latter comes to do his own will (Dan 11:36).

- The former glorified God on the earth (John 17:4); the latter blasphemes the name of God (Rev 13:6).

- The former is the good shepherd, who giveth his life for the sheep (John 10:14); the latter is the idol shepherd, who teareth the flock (Zech 11:16–17).

- The former was a man of sorrows (Isa 53:8); the latter is a king of fierce countenance (Dan 8:23).

- The former came not to destroy men's lives, but to save them (Luke 9:56); the latter shall destroy wonderfully, and shall prosper and practice, and shall destroy the mighty and the holy people (Dan 8:24).

- The former was meek and lowly in heart (Matt 11:29); the latter shall magnify himself in his heart (Dan 8:25).

- The former is the Prince of peace (Isa 9:6); the latter is the prince that shall come as a desolator (Dan 9:26–27).

- The former is the Lord from heaven (1 Cor 15:47); the latter is the man of the earth (Ps 10:18).

- The former is the true vine (John 15:1); the latter is the vine of the earth (Rev 14:18).

- The former was received up into heaven, and sat on the right hand of God (Mark 16:19); the latter goeth into perdition (Rev 17:8, 11).

These contrasts might be continued at considerable length, but perhaps enough has been said to show that the Antichrist is to be a real person.

- He will not appear until the ancient Roman empire reappears in the form of ten independent but confederated kingdoms (cf. Dan 7:21–24); but the Popes and Popery have already existed for centuries.

- He is to personify the godless culture of these last days, possessing rare intelligence, indicated by the fact that the horn of power which symbolized him "had eyes and a mouth that spake very great things" (Dan 7:20).

- He is to be a scholar of fine attainments, "understanding dark sentences" (Dan 8:23).

- He is to exult in the strength of his intellect, for "he shall exalt himself, and magnify himself above every God, and shall speak marvelous things against the God of gods" (Dan 11:36).

- He is to be a warrior of renown, for "'in his office shall he honor the God of fortresses" (Dan 11:38); and the wondering world will exclaim, "Who is able to make war with him?" (Rev 13:4).

As a man of transcendent genius, as a statesman of marvelous ability, as a politician of matchless skill, as a soldier born to command, it will be easy enough for the ten kingdoms to elect him their Imperator or Umpire for the decision of civil questions, their Generalissimo in the event of war, without disturbing their autonomy. These ten kingdoms, the Scriptures intimate, will largely manifest the character of a democracy, which without the fear of God, tends to lawlessness. Well, therefore, is the Antichrist called "the Lawless one," for he will give triumphant expression for a time to the lawlessness that already pervades all classes of society, children becoming more and more restless under parental authority, servants hating their masters, workingmen plotting against their employers, subjects rebelling against their rulers, citizens seeking the overthrow of their governments, and the criminal, and licentious, and infidel classes increasing with appalling rapidity.

An eminent statistician has announced in one of our leading magazines that "in 1850 there was one criminal in 3,442 of the population of this country; in 1860 there was one in 1,647; in 1870 there was one in 1,172, and in 1880 one in 860." That there has been no improvement since 1880 may be inferred from the fact that the leading newspaper in one of our large cities recently said:

> "An examination of the jail calendar is appalling, and the situation grows worse day by day. Here are some figures that cannot even be suspected of lying. They were obtained from Deputy Warden Soffel ... For the even year of 1889 there were 4,198 commitments to jail, or nearly one fifth of the total for seven years and six months. For eight

months and a half of the present year [1890], there have been 4,238, forty more than all of last year, and Mr. Soffel says the condition grows worse day by day."

Even in sober, staid Philadelphia, according to the *Record* of that city, there were 237 arrests of boys under 15 years of age in the month of January 1891, for burglary, larceny and other crimes.

Meanwhile the church, not only the Papal but the Protestant, is approaching the Laodicean state, which also implies lawlessness, the word meaning "the right, custom, usage, manner or fashion of the people." Boastful, proud and insolent, they do as they please, and to a lamentable extent vie with the world in their contempt of authority, human or divine.

Prominent professors in colleges and even in theological seminaries stand shoulder to shoulder with open infidels in their assaults upon the word of God. They deny its inspiration, authority, and authenticity. They sneer at the story of man's fall; they reject miracles; they ridicule prophecy; they scout the doctrine of future punishment; and in no respect do they differ from avowed skeptics except in the hollow and hypocritical profession of a name. Outside of professing Christianity, so profound a thinker as John Stuart Mill deliberately declared that "the God of the Bible should at least never extort from him the homage of love, to whatever else He might compel him;" and so influential a member of Parliament as John Morley describes God as "a Being no more entitled to our homage or worship than Francesco Cenci was entitled to the filial piety of his unhappy children;" while one of the greatest of England's living poets crowns the horrible blasphemy with the words:

"Thou art smitten, O God, Thou art smitten; Thy curse is upon Thee, O Lord!
And the love song of earth, as Thou diest, resounds through the wind of its wings,
Glory to man in the highest, for man is the master of things."

The people have been educated to reject with scorn the truth that "God was manifest in the flesh," and the next logical and unavoidable step is that "Man is God." The son of one of the most eminent preachers in America, himself a few years ago an apparently earnest and intelligent Christian, is now lecturing every Sunday in a hall to a crowd of renegade Christians, who have adopted as their motto, "Down with God; up with man;" and this beyond question is the popular demand. Inside of professing Christianity, there are comparatively few who are not "traitors, heady, high-minded, lovers of pleasures more than lovers of God; having a form of godliness, but denying the power thereof" (2 Tim 3:4–5); so that both a God-defying world and an apostate church, Papal and Protestant, are busily engaged in preparing the way for the advent of the Antichrist.

> What is our sweetest joy?
> Beloved companion, say;
> What our delightful, best employ,
> Untiring, free from all alloy,
> In this dark, cloudy day?
> To speak together of our home,
> Looking for Him who soon will come.

> Where do our spirits find
> Refreshment and repose?
> When heart to heart, and mind to mind,
> We search those records God designed,
> To medicine all our woes;
> And feel as bright, its pages shine,
> Each line was traced by Love divine.

We look on all around
As soon to disappear;
We listen to the tempest's sound,
As wildly now it sweeps around,
Without an anxious fear;
We hear a voice amidst its swell
Which whispers, "All will soon be well!"

Yes, soon the Lord will come;
Then will all trouble cease;
Earth's kingdoms will His own become;
Proud Antichrist will meet his doom;
All will be joy and peace:
These very storms prepare His way.
And usher in that glorious day.

8

Israel

The story is told of Frederick the Great that he abruptly said to his court chaplain, "give me an argument for the truth of the Bible in a single word." The man without a moment's hesitation replied, "Israel." The same word is the key that unlocks the meaning of the prophetic Scriptures, and those who do not see the place Israel occupies in God's word and in His purposes for the future, must at best go in a blundering way through the inspired writings. They are like the unbelieving Jews of whom the apostle speaks: "Their minds were blinded, for until this day remaineth the same vail untaken away in the reading of the Old Testament" (2 Cor 3:14).

From Moses to Malachi, and from Matthew to Revelation, there is abundant and unvarying testimony that the literal descendants of the literal Abraham and Isaac and Jacob, shall be literally scattered among all nations, as a punishment for their sins, and in the last days shall be literally restored to their own land, and rejoice once more in their covenant relations to Jehovah, as the head of the millennial nations. The passages affirming this are so numerous it would require a book of considerable size to reproduce them, nor can they be set aside by the idle fancy that they refer to the return of a few thousand Jews from the Babylonian captivity or that they are fulfilled spiritually to the church.

Long after the return from Babylon, the Lord Jesus said to the Jews, "Behold, your house is left unto you desolate. For I say unto you, ye shall not see me henceforth, till ye shall say, Blessed is He that cometh in the name of the Lord" (Matt 23:38–39). If this does not mean that they shall see Him again, and then they shall say, "Blessed is He that cometh in the name of the Lord," language has no meaning. The prediction did not relate to His appearance after His resurrection nor to the descent of the Spirit on the day of Pentecost, for in the first place they did not see Him but only His disciples. In the second place, they did not say, "Blessed is He that cometh in the name of the Lord." In the third place, their house was left unto them more desolate than before. It remains therefore to be fulfilled at Christ's second coming.

On another occasion our Lord said, "Jerusalem shall be trodden down of the Gentiles, until the times of the Gentiles be fulfilled" (Luke 21:24). Notwithstanding the malicious attempt of Julian, the apostate, and the tremendous efforts of the crusaders to defeat the prediction, Jerusalem continues to be trodden down of the Gentiles. But words have no significance if the word *until* does not point to a day when Jerusalem shall cease to be trodden down of the Gentiles, and handed back to the Jews, or become uninhabited.

In the only council of the apostles of which there is any record, James voiced the opinion of the others when he said, "Simeon [that is, Peter] hath declared how God at the first did visit the Gentiles, to take out of them a people for His name," or, as we would say, the church, the called-out ones, the *ecclesia*, "a Greek word," as Dr. Joseph Addison Alexander tells us, "which according to its etymology means something *called out* or evoked, and by implication *called together* or convoked, as a separate assembly or society, *selected from a greater number*." God never had any other purpose through the preaching of the gospel in the present age, or if He had, His purpose has been dreadfully baffled.

"And to this agree the words of the prophets," all of the prophets, although but one is quoted: "as it is written, After this I will return." After what? After He has taken out of the Gentiles a people for His name. "After this I will return," and when He says, "I will return," He means, I will return. When He returns, what will He do? "And will build again the tabernacle of David, which is fallen down; and I will build again the ruins thereof, and I will set it up." Once more, then, He will take poor Israel into covenant relationship with Himself, and with what object and result? "That the residue of men might seek after the Lord, and ALL the

Gentiles, upon whom my name is called, saith the Lord, who doeth all these things" (Acts 15:14–17).

We are not surprised, therefore, to find the Holy Ghost writing by the pen of Paul concerning Israel:

> "If the fall of them be the riches of the world, and the diminishing [decay or loss] of them the riches of the Gentiles, how much more their fulness? ... For if the casting away of them be the reconciling of the world, what shall the receiving of them be, but life from the dead? ... For I would not, brethren, that ye should be ignorant of this mystery, lest ye should be wise in your own conceits; that blindness [or hardness] in part has happened to Israel, until the fulness of the Gentiles be come in. And so all Israel shall be saved; as it is written, There shall COME out of Sion the Deliverer, and shall turn away ungodliness from Jacob" (Rom 11:12–26).

The fulness of the Gentiles means, of course, the complete number God takes out of the Gentiles to be "a people for His name," answering to "the times of the Gentiles," of which our Lord speaks (cf. Luke 21:24). So the divine procedure is as follows: first, the call of Israel; second, the call of the church; third, the setting aside of both for unfaithfulness; fourth, the personal return of the Lord; fifth, the salvation of all Israel; sixth, the salvation of all Gentiles, at least in outward confession; seventh, the millennial kingdom of a thousand years. Or, as the late Dr. Hugh McNeil well put it:

> "There are four steps in the conversion of the world: some Jews, some Gentiles, the nation of Israel, and the nations of the Gentiles. Some Jews, called 'a remnant according to the election of grace;' some Gentiles, called 'a people taken out for His name'—these are both one in Christ, and form

the church. Then the nation of Israel, on the return of the Lord; then the Gentile nations."

Hence we might expect to discover in the Old Testament the plainest and most explicit promises of Israel's restoration to their own land, and of their return into covenant relation and privilege and obligation as the peculiar people of Jehovah. The threat to scatter them among the Gentiles was literally executed; the promise to restore them will be as literally accomplished. "And yet for all that, when they be in the land of their enemies, I will not cast them away, neither will I abhor them, to destroy them utterly, and to break my covenant with them; for I am the Lord their God" (Lev 26:33, 44). This unconditional covenant, which was confirmed by oath and is therefore unchangeable, guarantees to them a specific body of land, mentioned again and again, that stretches from the river Nile, up the Mediterranean coast, and eastward to the Euphrates, 600 miles from north to south, and about 1,200 miles in its widest breadth, containing at least 300,000 square miles, and capable of supplying the wants of many millions of people. The Israelites have never yet possessed this vast territory, and as God is true they shall possess it hereafter.

In another passage, after a long chapter crowded with frightful woes, it was said to Israel, "If any of thine be driven out unto the utmost parts of heaven, from thence will the Lord thy God gather thee, and from thence will He fetch thee; and the Lord thy God will bring thee into the land which thy fathers possessed, and thou shalt possess it; and He will do thee good, and multiply thee above thy fathers" (Deut 30:4–5). Similar passages are found in abundance:

- "Thy people also shall be all righteous; they shall inherit the land forever" (Isa 60:21).

- Of Jerusalem God says, "it shall not be plucked up, nor thrown down, any more forever" (Jer 31:40; cf. 31:31–40).

- "In those days shall Judah be saved, and Jerusalem shall dwell safely; and this is the name whereby she shall be called, The Lord our Righteousness" (Jer 33:16; cf. 33:15–26).

- "Thus saith the Lord God, I will even gather you from the people, and assemble you out of the countries where ye have been scattered, and I will give you the land of Israel" (Ezek 11:17; cf. 11:16–20).

- "The children of Israel shall abide many days without a king, and without a prince, and without a sacrifice, and without an image [margin, standing], and without an ephod, and without teraphim. Afterward shall the children of Israel *return*, and seek the Lord their God, and David their King, and shall fear the Lord and His goodness *in the latter days*" (Hos 3:4–5).

The Jewish Rabbi Kimchi strikingly says:

> "These are the days of the captivity in which we now are at this day; we have *no king nor prince* out of Israel, for we are in the power of the nations and of their kings and princes; and have *no sacrifice* for God, *nor image* for idols; *no ephod* for God that declares future things by Urim and Thummim, and *no teraphim* for idols, which show things to come, according to the mind of those that believe in them."

Other passages could be included:

- "Ye shall know that I am in the midst of Israel, and that I am the Lord your God, and none else, and my people shall never be ashamed. And it shall come to pass *afterward* that I will pour out my Spirit upon all flesh" (Joel 2:27–28).

- "I will bring again the captivity of my people of Israel, and they shall build the waste cities, and inhabit them; and they shall plant vineyards, and drink the wine thereof; they shall make gardens, and eat the fruit of them. And I will plant them upon their land, and they shall no more be pulled out of their land, which I have given them, saith the Lord God" (Amos 9:14–15).

- "Behold, the days come, saith the Lord, that I will sow the house of Israel, and the house of Judah, with the seed of man, and with the seed of beast. And it shall come to pass, that like as I have watched over them, to pluck up, and to break down, and to throw down, and to destroy, and to afflict; so will I watch over them, to build and to plant, saith the Lord" (Jer 31:27–28).

There are scores upon scores of similar statements, equally plain and positive in the promise that the literal seed of Jacob shall in the latter days be returned to the land which God gave to their fathers. But how do we know that the promises do not refer to the return from Babylon? Because they look to a second restoration, and because since that time Israel has been plucked up out of the land.

> "It shall come to pass in that day, that the Lord shall set His hand again the second time to recover the remnant of His people; ... and he shall set up an ensign for the nations, and shall assemble the outcasts of Israel and gather together the dispersed of Judah *from the four corners of the earth*. The envy also of Ephraim shall depart, and the adversaries of Judah shall be cut off; Ephraim shall not envy Judah, and Judah shall not vex Ephraim" (Isa 11:11–13).

> "Thus saith the Lord God, behold, I will take the children
> of Israel from among the heathen, whither they be gone,
> and will gather them on every side, and bring them into
> their own land: and I will make them one nation in the
> land upon the mountains of Israel, and one King shall be
> King to them all, and they shall be no more two nations
> [Judah and the ten tribes], neither shall they be divided
> into two kingdoms any more at all" (Ezek 37:21–22).

There are many similar statements which the reader is entreated to
look up for himself; and, if the subject is new to him, he will be amazed
at the number of clear, explicit, unconditional predictions of Israel's
restoration to the land, and to the favor of Jehovah, which has been
utterly forfeited.

> "I will take you from among the heathen, and gather you
> out of all countries, and will bring you into your own
> land.... Ye shall dwell in the land that I gave to your fa-
> thers; and ye shall be my people, and I will be your God....
> Not for your sakes do I this, saith the Lord God, be it
> known unto you: be ashamed and confounded for your
> own ways, O house of Israel" (Ezek 36:24–28, 32).

It is grace all the way through, and therefore, "He that scattered Israel
will gather him, and keep him, as a shepherd doth his flock" (Jer 31:10).
If the scattering is literal, so is the gathering. Israel and Jerusalem are
mentioned hundreds of times in the Bible, and in every instance they
mean the natural posterity of Jacob and the capital of Judah, except in
the two or three verses where we read "Above," "Heavenly," "New," as
descriptive of a spiritual city.

Israel, however, will be brought to God only through terrible judgments.

- "Thus saith the Lord God, because ye are all become dross, behold, therefore, I will gather you into the midst of Jerusalem. As they gather silver, and brass, and iron, and lead, and tin, into the midst of the fire to blow upon it, to melt it; so will I gather you in my anger and in my fury, and I will leave you there, and melt you" (Ezek 22:19–20).

- "Alas! for that day is great, so that none is like it; it is even the time of Jacob's trouble; but he shall be saved out of it" (Jer 30:7).

- "And at that time shall Michael stand up, the great prince that standeth for the children of thy people; and there shall be a time of trouble, such as never was since there was a nation even to that same time; and at that time thy people shall be delivered, every one that shall be found written in the book" (Dan 12:1).

- "I will gather all nations against Jerusalem to battle; and the city shall be taken, and the houses rifled, and the women ravished; and half the city shall go forth in captivity, and the residue of the people shall not be cut off from the city. Then shall the Lord go forth, and fight against those nations, as when He fought in the day of battle. And His feet shall stand in that day upon the mount of Olives, which is before Jerusalem on the east; ... and the Lord my God shall come, and all the saints with Him.... And the Lord shall be King over all the earth: in that day shall there be one Lord, and His name one" (Zech 14:1–9).

In the time of Jacob's trouble Antichrist will play a conspicuous part.

- "He shall speak great words against the Most High, and shall wear out the saints of the Most High, and think to change times and laws: and they shall be given into his hand, until a time, and times, and the dividing of time" (Dan 7:25).

- "He shall confirm a covenant with many for one heptad, and in the midst of the heptad [leaving 3.5 years, 1,260 days, forty and two months, a time, times, and the dividing of time] he shall cause the sacrifice and oblation to cease, and upon the battlements shall be the idols of the desolator, even until the consummation, and that determined shall be poured upon the desolator" (Dan 9:27).

- He will invade the land at the head of an immense host; but it is said to him, "Thou shalt fall upon the mountains of Israel, thou, and all thy bands, and the people that is with thee: I will give thee unto the ravenous birds of every sort, and to the beasts of the field; to be devoured" (Ezek 39:4).

At the appearing of the KING OF KINGS, AND LORD OF LORDS, a call is made to all the fowls that fly in the midst of heaven, "Come and gather yourselves together unto the supper of the great God; that ye may eat the flesh of kings, and the flesh of captains, and the flesh of mighty men, and the flesh of horses" (Rev 19:16–18). The name of Jerusalem "from that day shall be The Lord is there" (Ezek 48:35). Then, too, "He shall cause them that come of Jacob to take root: Israel shall blossom and bud, and fill the face of the earth with fruit" (Isa 27:6).

No one can read the word of God with an unprejudiced mind, and with a sincere desire to know the truth, without seeing that the salvation of Israel has a direct bearing upon the salvation of the world. We hear the cry of Israel, "God be merciful unto US, and bless US, and cause His face to shine upon US," and what then? "That Thy way may be known upon earth, Thy saving health among all people.... God shall bless US; and all the ends of the earth shall fear Him" (Ps 67:1–7). So we are plainly told that "when the Lord shall build up Zion, He shall APPEAR in His glory." But for what purpose? "To declare the name of the Lord in Zion, and His praise in Jerusalem; when the people are gathered together, and the kingdoms, to serve the Lord" (Ps 102:21–22).

He therefore is doing most to hasten the universal triumph of the cross, who most literally obeys the injunction of the Holy Ghost, "Pray for the peace of Jerusalem: they shall prosper that love thee" (Ps 122:6). The promise shall surely be fulfilled to the daughter of Zion, "unto thee shall it come, even the first dominion; the kingdom shall come to the daughter of Jerusalem" (Mic 4:8). It is strange that brethren who deny the literal restoration of Israel do not see that God must have preserved this extraordinary people for some wonderful purpose.

For 2500 years the four great world empires, and the kingdoms of Christendom, have sought to crush them, and at this day the most gigantic despotism of earth is trying to grind them to powder. But all of this is but the outworking of Jehovah's plans, "till He make Jerusalem a praise in the earth" (Isa 62:7), when "ten men shall take hold, out of all languages of the nations, even shall take hold of the skirt of him that is a Jew, saying, We will go with you; for we have heard that God is with you" (Zech 8:23). "Then the moon shall be confounded, and the sun ashamed, when the Lord of hosts shall reign in mount Zion, and in Jerusalem, and before His ancients, gloriously" (Isa 24:23). Even now the God of Abraham and of Isaac and of Jacob, the covenant keeping God, is preparing the way for the return of their posterity to the land of their fathers. From twenty to fifty Jewish families are landed every week at Jaffa, and the four lines of steamers from Constantinople and Russian ports are crowded with refugees who have already taken possession of Jerusalem. In the increasing fertility of the soil, and in the remarkable return of the chosen people, God is beginning to give back to them, although still blind, "the City of the great King" (Matt 5:35).

"Rejoice ye with Jerusalem!
Tier night of tears is o'er;
Now comes her hour of glorious power,
And splendor evermore;
Rejoice ye with Jerusalem!
City of peace and light;
Her morn at last is breaking fast,
And ended is her night.
Her widow's weeds are gone,
Her royal robes put on.

Ye who have read upon her walls
The guilt, the curse, the shame,
Now full in view see fair and new
Her everlasting name.
Ye who have read upon her towers
The vengeance from above,
Read now in light the sentence bright
Of pardon and of love.
Forgiven and comforted,
She lifts her joyful head.

The sun of earth she needeth not,
Nor asks his light again;
Jehovah is her Sun of bliss
Her God her glory then.
Her moon again shall never wane,
Nor shall her sun descend,
Her storms are done, her calm begun,
Her mourning is at end.
Her long, long fast is done,
Her long, long feast begun."

9

The Rapture

The question now to be discussed touches vitally the entire subject of our Lord's second advent. Many beloved and excellent brethren hold that there is no perceptible interval between His coming *for* His people and His appearing *with* them. They believe, therefore, that the church, the true church, the regenerated ones who are seeking to walk in fellowship with Christ, and in separation from evil, must pass through the terrible tribulation under the Antichrist in the last days, before they are caught up in clouds to meet the Lord in the air. But there is strong ground for very serious objections to this theory, whatever affection and respect may be due to those by whom it is advanced.

In the first place, it renders null and void all the commands of the Saviour, and of His apostles, to look for His coming as possible any day. It cannot be denied that we are to be watching for His return at evening, at midnight, at the cock crowing, and morning (Mark 13:36–37). It cannot be denied that every real believer is to be like a faithful servant standing at the hall door with girded loins and burning lights, peering through the outer darkness for the first gleam of His advancing glory, and listening with attentive ear for the faintest echo of His approaching steps (cf. Luke 12:35–36). It cannot be denied that the Christians of the apostles' times were taught to wait for God's Son from heaven (1 Thess 1:10), and were found "waiting for the coming of our Lord Jesus Christ" (1 Cor 1:7). But if He cannot come until the restoration of the Jews in large numbers to Jerusalem, until the division of the old Roman empire into ten kingdoms, to be followed by the appearing of the Antichrist, it is useless to be looking for Him now. Beyond question, according to the teachings of the New Testament from Matthew to the close of Revelation, it is the proper posture of the soul to be expecting Him every hour, as we need Him "every hour," and that cannot be a true doctrine which disturbs this beautiful posture, and makes it impossible.

In the second place, it will not be denied that when our Lord appears on this earth, His saints shall appear with Him.

- "The Lord my God shall come, and all the saints with Him" (Zech 14:5).

- "When Christ, who is our life, shall appear, then shall ye also appear with Him in glory" (Col 3:4).

- "At the coming of our Lord Jesus Christ with all His saints" (1 Thess 3:13).

- "If we believe that Jesus died and rose again, even so them also which sleep in Jesus will God bring with Him" (1 Thess 4:14).

- "Behold, the Lord cometh with ten thousands of His saints" (Jude 14).

- "The armies which were in heaven followed Him upon white horses, clothed in line linen, white and clean" (Rev 19:14), and "the fine linen is the righteousness of saints" (Rev 19:8), and "they that are with Him are called, and chosen, and faithful" (Rev 17:14), identifying them with saved men from the earth.

Such passages teach beyond doubt that those who are manifested with Him at His advent must have been previously caught up unto Him; and a sufficient length of time must have elapsed to reckon with His servants, according to their faithfulness (cf. Matt 24:14–24; Luke 19:12–19), and to be judged according to the deeds done in the body (2 Cor 5:10); because when He finally appears they shall be associated with Him in the administration of His kingdom: "Do ye not know that the saints shall judge the world?" (1 Cor 6:2)?

In the third place, our Lord plainly promises to keep His watchful ones out of the tribulation. Speaking of that tribulation, when there shall be "upon the earth distress of nations, with perplexity; the sea and the waves roaring, men's hearts failing them for fear, and for looking after those things which are coming on the earth" (Luke 21:25–26), He says to His disciples, "Take heed to yourselves, lest AT ANY TIME your hearts be overcharged with surfeiting, and drunkenness, and cares of this life, and so that day come upon you unawares. For as a snare shall it come on all them that dwell [are settled down] on the face of the whole earth. Watch ye, therefore, and pray always, that ye may be accounted worthy to escape all these things that shall come to pass, and to stand before the Son of man" (Luke 21:34–36). Again He promises still more explicitly, "Because thou hast kept the word of my patience, I also will keep thee from [out of] the hour of temptation, which shall come upon all the world, to try them that dwell upon the earth" (Rev 3:10). Here, then, is the positive assurance that the faithful shall be kept, not by His power *through* the tribulation, but *out of* the hour, elsewhere rendered "time" and "season," of the tribulation, that shall burst like a storm upon all the world.

In the fourth place, after the Laodicean or last state of professing Christendom, when lukewarm indifference and pride and boasting prevail, and Christ is excluded from His own house (Rev 3), the church is seen no more upon the earth, until she appears in Revelation 19, following her Bridegroom from heaven. On the other hand, the representatives of the redeemed, are in heaven. The entire interval between the close of the church age and the marriage supper of the Lamb is filled with appalling judgments, and the whole scene is intensely Jewish, as shown in the sealing of the "hundred and forty and four thousand of all the tribes of the children of Israel" (Rev 7:4), the temple, the court of the Gentiles, and the testimony of the two witnesses, who like the Old Testament prophets, devour their enemies with fire, and have power to shut heaven, that it rain not, and have power over waters to turn them to blood, and to smite the earth with all plagues. There is not a hint that the church is here during the period of awful tribulation; and even the Holy Spirit is not viewed as officially upon the earth, but takes His place before the throne (cf. Rev 1:4; 4:5; 5:6).

In the fifth place, we are distinctly taught that when our Lord leaves the right hand of the throne of God, He pauses long enough in the air to gather His risen and translated saints around Himself. "The Lord Himself shall descend from heaven with a shout, ... and the dead in Christ shall rise first; then we which are alive and remain, shall be caught up together with them in the clouds, to meet the Lord in the air" (1 Thess 4:16–17). Apart from the fact that the word "shout" is, as Canon Fausset renders it, "a signal shout," a military call and command to His own, with which others have no concern; and apart from the fact that the word "meet," wherever else it occurs in the New Testament, implies a meeting so as to return with the person met, it is certain that there are two stages in our Lord's second advent. He comes into the air, and there summons His own to meet Him, and then He comes with them to the earth. There are not two comings, but two steps of one coming, as there were two steps of His first coming, the one at Bethlehem and the other at Calvary. It is not stated in so many words how long the pause in the air will be, nor why it occurs, but it may be inferred from many Scriptures that it will continue for seven years, during the manifestation of the Antichrist's power.

In the sixth place, the analogy of Scriptures favors the twofold aspect in which the second advent is to be viewed. There is a personal and invisible relation of truth to God, and an open and outward manifestation of it to the world. We are justified before God without works of any kind (Rom 4:5), but we are justified before men by our works (James 2:24). We are sanctified before God now" (1 Cor 6:11), but we are sanctified before men progressively (1 Thess 4:3; 5:23). The Holy Spirit always dwells in the believer as he stands before God (John 14:17), but the Holy Spirit comes upon him for service and testimony before men (Acts 1:8). The believer shall not come into judgment as to his sins (John 5:24), but the believer must appear before the judgment seat of Christ as to his works (2 Cor 5:10). There is to be a resurrection of the just in glorified bodies, and hence Paul's earnest desire, "if by any means I might attain unto the resurrection of the dead" (Phil 3:11), but there is to be a resurrection of the unjust a thousand years afterwards (Rev 20:5). We might expect, therefore, to find that there is to be a coming of the Lord for His people, and then, whether the delay is long or short, His appearing with them, thus bringing the two phases of the second advent into harmony with other great doctrines.

In the seventh place, He has shown us that the rapture or translation is to be secret and unknown to the world, and that His summons to His own will not be heard, or at least not understood, by the unbelieving mass. "Enoch walked with God; and he was not, for God took him" (Gen 5:24), and no man saw him ascend; but he was kept out of the hour of temptation, while Noah passed safely through the tribulation. When Elijah was caught away in a chariot of fire, only Elisha saw it, and the sons of the prophets searched in vain for the missing messenger of Jehovah. Jesus on His way to the cross cried, "Father, glorify Thy name. Then came there a voice from heaven, saying, I have both glorified it, and will glorify it again." This was distinct enough to His ear, but the people that stood by said "that it thundered" (John 12:28–29). Paul on his way to Damascus heard the words of our risen and ascended Lord, "I am Jesus, whom thou persecutest.... Arise, and go into the city, and it shall be told thee what thou must do. And the men which journeyed with him stood speechless, hearing a voice, but seeing no man" (Acts 9:4–7). Afterward Paul said, "They that were with me saw indeed the light, and were afraid; but they heard not the voice of Him that spake to me" (Acts 22:9).

Is there then a contradiction here, as infidels in and out of the church have been saying for centuries? No greater contradiction that when persons, listening to a speaker in a large audience, assert that they do not hear him, although his voice fills the building. It needs a circumcised ear and a circumcised heart to hear the words of the Lord, since "the natural man receiveth not the things of the Spirit of God: for they are foolishness unto him; neither can he know them, because they are spiritually discerned" (1 Cor 2:14). Even if the shout of our descending Lord is heard by the unbelieving world, it will not be heard in the scriptural sense of the word; and no doubt many a jest and scientific guess will appear in the newspapers about the strange sound in the sky, none but the elect knowing that it called His waiting and watching ones to meet Him in the air.

- He comes into the air as the Bridegroom (Matt 25:6).

- He comes to the earth as the Nobleman who "went into a far country to receive for Himself a Kingdom, and to return" (Luke 19:12).

- He comes into the air as "The Morning Star" (Rev 22:16).

- He comes to the earth as "The Sun of Righteousness" (Mal 4:2).

- He comes into the air to present the church to Himself, all glorious (Eph 5:27).

- He comes to the earth to overthrow the armies of all nations gathered against Jerusalem to battle (Zech 14:2–3).

- He comes into the air in blessed fulfillment of the promise, I will "receive you unto Myself" (John 14:3).

- He comes to the earth as KING OF KINGS, AND LORD OF LORDS (Rev 19:16).

- He comes into the air to celebrate "the marriage supper of the Lamb" (Rev 19:9).

- He comes to the earth to prepare "the supper of the great God" (Rev 19:17).

- He comes into the air to bring His faithful ones to the banqueting house, where His banner over them is love (Song 2:4).

- He comes to the earth to give them power over the nations, and they shall rule them with a rod of iron; as the vessels of a potter shall they be broken to shivers (Rev 2:26–27).

- He comes into the air for the joy of His followers (John 16:22).

- He comes to the earth to judge the nations (Matt 25:31–32; Acts 17:31).

There is no predicted event between this passing moment and His coming; into the air, but much remains to be fulfilled before He comes to the earth. It would be scriptural to say, the Lord *may* come today, or tomorrow, or next week, or next month, or next year; it would be unscriptural to say, the Lord *will not* come today, nor tomorrow, nor next week, nor next month, nor next year. If to the statement it is objected that He Himself tells us, "This gospel of the kingdom shall be preached in all the world for a witness unto all nations, and then shall the end come" (Matt 24:14), it is a sufficient answer to reply that the Father alone has authority to determine when this testimony to His Son shall have been sufficiently borne (Acts 1:7); and since it is revealed that after our Lord's coming to the earth, the saved of Israel shall rush as His ambassadors to the isles that are afar off, that have not heard His fame, nor seen His glory (Isa 66:19), it is certain that the gospel will not have been preached to every creature before His coming into the air.

The fact is that we of this church dispensation have nothing to do with signs and dates, and it is dangerous and delusive to get our thoughts fixed upon these. It is most important to remember that the Holy Spirit takes notice of "times and seasons" only with respect to Israel. Those who form the body of the risen Christ, and are "partakers of the heavenly calling," are timeless people, and need not study history. We are like an army when the general issues his orders, "Be ready to move at a moment's notice." Every inferior officer, and every soldier must be instantly prepared, and continue in a state of preparation, no matter how long the notice may be deferred, until the order to march is received. The Captain of our salvation has commanded us to wait and to watch, and it is not for us to be interposing certain events, nor to be looking around for fulfilled prophecy, before expecting to hear His order bidding us mount up in clouds to meet Him in the air. Nay, our rapture may be quicker than the twinkling of an eye (1 Cor 15:52), for that means the closing and uplifting of the eyelid, but the Greek word may imply a single movement. O sweet thought! here one moment, and the next, like a flash, with the Lord. "Be ye therefore ready also: for the Son of man cometh at an hour when ye think not" (Luke 12:40).

> I'm waiting for Thee, Lord,
> Thy beauty to see, Lord,
> I'm waiting for Thee,
> For Thy coming again.
> Thou'rt gone over there, Lord,
> A place lo prepare, Lord;
> Thy home I shall share,
> At Thy coming again.
>
> Mid danger and fear, Lord,
> I'm oft weary here, Lord;
> The day must be near
> Of Thy coming again.
> 'Tis all sunshine there, Lord,
> No sighing nor care, Lord,
> But glory so fair
> At Thy coming again.
>
> Whilst Thou art away, Lord,
> I stumble and stray, Lord;
> Oh, hasten the day Of Thy coming again.
> This is not my rest, Lord,
> A pilgrim confest, Lord,
> I wait to be blest
> At Thy coming again.

Our loved ones before, Lord,
Their troubles are o'er, Lord;
I'll meet them once more
At Thy coming again.
The blood was the sign, Lord,
That marked them as Thine, Lord,
And brightly they'll shine
At Thy coming again.

E'en now let my ways, Lord,
Be bright with Thy praise, Lord,
For brief are the days
Ere Thy coming again.
I'm waiting for Thee, Lord,
Thy beauty to see, Lord,
No triumph for me
Like Thy coining again.

10

That Blessed Hope

There are three things which grace does for the believer. It saves, it teaches, and it holds out "a sure and certain hope" to animate the redeemed and instructed pilgrim on his way to meet the Lord in the air.

> "The grace of God that bringeth salvation hath appeared to all men, teaching us, that, denying ungodliness and worldly lusts, we should live soberly, righteously and godly, in this present world, looking for that blessed hope, even the glorious appearing of our great God and Saviour Jesus Christ, who gave Himself for us, that He might redeem us from all iniquity, and purify unto Himself a peculiar people, zealous of good works" (Titus 2:11–14).

"These things speak," adds the apostle, including, among the things the faithful minister is to speak, "that blessed hope."

A glance at the Scriptures will be sufficient to show why it is called that blessed hope, and why Christians are represented as looking or waiting for it with eager expectation. Grace shines in our salvation, but there will be a shining forth of glory at the second coming of Christ, while between the first and the last step we are kept by the power of God, fulfilling the promise of the word, "The Lord God is a sun and shield; the Lord will give grace and glory" (Ps 84:11). If the return of our Saviour from the heavens could be seen as a happy hope, not as a terrible trial, no doubt many who now shrink from all mention of the subject would speak of it with exultant hearts and longing desire.

First, consider the bearing of the second advent upon the creation around us.

> "The earnest expectation of the creature [or creation] waiteth [to watch with the head stretched out] for the manifestation of the sons of God. For the creation was made subject to vanity, not willingly, but by reason of him who hath subjected the same in hope; because the creation itself also shall be delivered from the bondage of corruption into the glorious liberty of the children of God. For we know that the whole creation groaneth and travaileth together in pain until now. And not only they, but ourselves also, which have the firstfruits of the Spirit, even we ourselves groan within ourselves, awaiting for the adoption, the redemption of our body" (Rom 8:19–23).

Prof. Beet says:

> "The *Creation* is especially distinguished from the children of God, and therefore does not include them. The words 'subject' and 'groan' exclude the happy spirits of other worlds. The coming liberation excludes bad angels, and those who finally reject the gospel. For to the latter the *coming of Christ* will bring wrath [Rom 2:8], and we cannot conceive it to bring liberty to the former. It remains therefore that the word denotes the entire world around us, living and without life, man alone excepted. It is what we call nature, but reminds us that nature is the work of God."

Dr. Charles Hodge takes the same view, and tells us, "The manifestation of the sons of God is a definite Scriptural event, just as much as the second advent of Christ," and "the time of the resurrection of the body or the manifestation of the sons of God, is the time of the second advent of Jesus Christ." With this all expositors of all schools cordially agree.

It follows, therefore, that creation or nature cannot cease from its groans and travailing throes until the second advent of Jesus Christ. Then, however, "the wilderness and the solitary place shall be glad for them; and the desert shall rejoice and blossom as the rose" (Isa 35:1). Then "the mountains and the hills shall break forth before you into singing, and all the trees of the field shall clap their hands" (Isa 55:12). There are many similar statements in the Scriptures that lose all their significance and beauty for multitudes, because they are dismissed from the mind with the flippant remark that they are figurative and poetical. Suppose they are figurative and poetical; they are not lies, for the word of God contains no lie, and hence a glorious change awaits the now suffering creation at the second advent of Christ. If the figure or poetry is so enchanting, what must be the reality!

Second, consider the bearing of the second advent upon the lower animals.

> "The wolf also shall dwell with the lamb, and the leopard shall lie down with the kid; and the calf, and the young lion and the fatling together; and a little child shall lead them. And the cow and the bear shall feed; their young ones shall lie down together, and the lion shall eat straw like the ox. And the sucking child shall play on the hope of the asp, and the weaned child shall put his hand in the cockatrice den. They shall not hurt nor destroy in all my holy mountain, for the earth shall be full of the knowledge of the Lord, as the waters cover the sea" (Isa 11:6–9).

The same truth is set forth, among other places (cf. Isa 65:25; Ezek 34:25; Hos 2:18). That this lovely scene cannot be witnessed before the personal return of the Lord, is shown by the fact that it is introduced with the statement, "He shall smite the earth with the rod of His mouth, and with the breath of His lips shall He slay the wicked one" (Isa 11:4), precisely the phraseology that describes His visible coming in 2 Thessalonians 2:8.

Here again we are met with the objection that the language is figurative and poetical, and cannot mean what it says, the scientific ones among the brethren arguing that a lion's teeth are not adapted to grass eating. True, nor is a man's, and yet "the same hour was the thing fulfilled upon Nebuchadnezzar, and he was driven from men and did eat grass as oxen" (Dan 4:38). He who made the teeth can adapt the teeth to any purpose He pleases, and He who said to fallen Adam, "Cursed is the ground for thy sake" (Gen 3:17), can remove the curse, as He will do at the second coming of Christ, when the poor dumb beasts, so long the helpless victims of inhuman brutality and ruthless murder, will have the cruel yoke broken from their necks, and cease to fight with their tyrant and with one another.

Third, consider the bearing of the second advent upon civil governments. "He shall judge among the nations, and shall rebuke many people; and they shall beat their swords into plowshares and their spears into pruninghooks; nation shall not lift up sword against nation, neither shall they learn war any more" (Isa 2:4). This testimony is so important that it is reproduced by the Holy Ghost in another prophet (cf. Mic 4:3); and a pious Roman Catholic, who wrote over the signature of Ben Ezra, in a remarkable work called the "Coming of Messiah in Glory and Majesty," translated from the Spanish by Edward Irving, well says:

> "In the first place I sincerely agree with all the doctors, both Christian and Jewish, that the times of Messiah are manifestly the times spoken of in this prophecy. 'It shall come to pass in the last days,' that is, in the time of Messiah, or of Christ. Therefore the prophecy, and many others like it, which have not been verified, nor could possibly have been, in the first advent of the Messiah, may very

well and must needs be verified in the second, which time
is not less of divine faith than the first.... When then the
second advent, which we all religiously believe and expect,
is arrived, there shall be, among other things, primary
or principal, the elevation of Mount Zion above all the
mountains and hills, a manifestly figurative expression, yet
admirably proper to explain the dignity, honor and glory
to which the city of David shall then be lifted up; after
that the throne or tabernacle of David, which is fallen
down, shall have been set up and reestablished therein, 'as
in the days of old;' ... in which time consequently shall the
nations and peoples flow toward the top of Mount Zion.
What nation and peoples? Without doubt those who shall
be left after the coming of the Lord."

Fourth, consider the bearing of the second advent upon scattered
Israel. To the daughter of Zion and to the daughter of Jerusalem it is
said:

"The King of Israel, even the Lord, is in the midst of thee;
thou shalt not see evil any more. In that day it shall he
said to Jerusalem, Fear thou not; and to Zion, Let not
thine hands be slack. The Lord thy God in the midst
of thee is mighty; He will save, He will rejoice over thee
with joy; He will rest in His love; He will joy over thee
with singing. I will gather them that are sorrowful for the
solemn assembly, who are of thee, to whom the reproach
of it was a burden. Behold, at that time I will undo all that
afflict thee; and I will save her that halteth, and gather her
that was driven out; and I will get them praise and fame
in every land where they have been put to shame. At that
time [at the time when the King of Israel even the Lord,
is seen in the midst of the Jews], will I bring you again,
even in the time that I gather you, for I will make you a

name and a praise among all people of the earth, when I turn back your captivity before your eyes, saith the Lord" (Zeph 3:15–20).

Fifth, consider the bearing of the second advent upon sickness. "The inhabitant shall not say, I am sick" (Isa 33:24); and the context shows that this shall be a time when "thine eyes shall see the King in His beauty; they shall behold a far stretching land" (Isa 33:17, Revised Version).

> "There shall be no more thence an infant of days, nor an old man that hath not filled his days: for the child shall die a hundred years old; but the sinner, being a hundred years old, shall be accursed. And they shall build houses and inhabit them; and they shall plant vineyards, and eat the fruit of them. They shall not build and another inhabit; they shall not plant and another eat; for as the days of a tree are the days of my people, and mine elect shall long enjoy the work of their hands" (Isa 65:20–22).

This is an earthly, not a heavenly scene, for death is not wholly extinct, but it is exceptional, appearing only as a judicial infliction. Man will then fill his days, which he never yet has done, nor even Methuselah before the deluge. But then the righteous will live upon the earth for a thousand years, when the Lord reigns for a thousand years, and so long will be human life that one dying a hundred years old will be but a child, dying too, under some special curse.

Sixth, consider the bearing of the second advent upon the state of our dead.

> "I would not have you to be ignorant, brethren, concerning them which are asleep, that ye sorrow not, even as others that have no hope. For if we believe that Jesus died and rose again, even so them also which sleep in Jesus will

God bring with Him. For this we say unto you by the
word of the Lord, that we which are alive and remain unto
the coming of the Lord, shall not precede them which are
asleep. For the Lord Himself shall descend from heaven
with a shout, with the voice of the archangel, and with the
trump of God; and the dead in Christ shall rise first; then
we which are alive and remain shall be caught up together
with them in the clouds, to meet the Lord in the air. And
so shall we ever be with the Lord. Wherefore comfort one
another with these words" (1 Thess 4:13–18).

Where else shall we find comfort when our hearts are bursting over the
graves of our darlings, whom we shall see no more in the body "till He
come?" Oh, it is then and there a new meaning is given to the precious
promise, "Surely I come quickly. Amen." And the sorrowing soul calls
back with irrepressible longing, "Even so, come, Lord Jesus."

Seventh, consider the bearing of the second advent upon the conversion of the world. It is when Israel are back in their own land, and know
that the Messiah Lord is in the midst of them, and they shall never be
ashamed, the promise is fulfilled, "It shall come to pass AFTERWARD,
that I will pour out my Spirit upon all flesh" (Joel 2:28). It is when
He returns, and builds again the tabernacle of David, which is fallen
down, the residue of men seek after the Lord, "and all the Gentiles"
(Acts 15:14–17). It is after the sealing of the hundred and forty and four
thousand of all the tribes of the children of Israel, the apostle beheld,
and, lo, a great multitude, which no man could number, came out of the
tribulation, the great one, under Antichrist, having washed their robes
and made them white in the blood of the Lamb (Rev 7). They are not
the church, for Christ has already come to call the real church to heaven
as His bride, and she shall descend with Him. "Do ye not know that the
saints shall judge the world?" (1 Cor 6:2).

It is not strange, therefore, that the glorious epiphany of the great God,
our Saviour Jesus Christ, is called "that blessed hope." But it is strange
and sad beyond expression that every true Christian does not cry out for

His coming with continual desire, when we find that such a flood tide of
honor and glory and praise shall flash before His throne at His advent,
that such heights of blessedness shall then be attained by ourselves, and
that we are so hopeless without it.

> The Church has waited long
> Her absent Lord to see;
> And still in loneliness she waits;
> A friendless stranger she.
> Age after age has gone,
> Sun after sun has set,
> And still in weeds of widowhood
> She weeps a mourner yet.
> Come, then. Lord Jesus, come.
>
> Saint after saint on earth
> Has lived, and loved, and died;
> And as they left us one by one,
> We laid them side by side;
> We laid them down to sleep,
> But not in hope forlorn;
> We laid them but to ripen there.
> Till the last glorious morn.
> Come, then. Lord Jesus, come.
>
> We long to hear Thy voice,
> To see Thee face to face,
> To share Thy crown and glory then,
> As now we share Thy grace.
> Should not the loving bride,
> The absent Bridegroom mourn?
> Should she not wear the weeds of grief
> Until the Lord return?
> Come, then, Lord Jesus, come.

The whole creation groans,
And waits to hear that voice,
That shall restore her comeliness,
And make her wastes rejoice.
Come, Lord, and wipe away
The curse, the sin, the stain,
And make this blighted world of ours
Thine own fair world again.
Come, then, Lord Jesus, come.

11

The Only Hope

Whenever and wherever man has been placed in a position of responsibility he has failed. Thus we find him in the garden of Eden, radiant with beauty, surrounded by everything that could make him perfectly happy, and subjected to a simple test of obedience. But he believed the devil's lie, rather than God's truth, and was sent forth to till a sin-cursed earth in the sweat of his face, and to crumble back to dust. "Through one man sin entered into the world, and death through sin" (Rom 5:12). Never again can he be tried under circumstances so favorable; and the first trial, the dispensation of Innocence, ended in utter disaster and ruin.

This was followed by the dispensation of Conscience. There was no pronounced or written law, but he was left to his own sense of right and wrong to govern and judge his conduct. The result of the experiment is stated in the words, "God saw that the wickedness of man was great in the earth, and that every imagination of the thoughts of his heart was only evil continually" (Gen 6:5). "Every," "only," "evil," and "continually," tell the sad story of deep-seated depravity and wide-spread departure from their Creator. There must have been millions of people on the earth at the time the wrath of God was let loose in a flood to destroy the race; but out of all this vast multitude there was but one righteous man, who, with his household, was saved. So the second trial ended in utter disaster and ruin.

Then came the dispensation of the Family. Scarcely had the waters of the deluge subsided, before man in his defiance of God determined to build a tower that might reach unto heaven. Although confounded in his folly, he soon forgot the destruction of the world and the overthrow of Babel, and relapsed into the former iniquity, until universal idolatry covered the earth. Terah, the father of Abraham, was an idolater when his son was called out from his country and kindred, to train his household in the knowledge of the true God. The most intimate and precious relations were established between Jehovah and one who is three times called His friend, but we find the posterity of this friend in the lime kilns of Egypt, making bricks and groaning in the degradation of their slavery, and steeped in ignorance and unbelief. So the third trial ended in utter disaster and ruin.

Next we have the dispensation of the Law, when an entire nation was separated from all other nations, and told how to dress, and what to eat, and when to observe their religious rites, and where to worship, the utmost pains being taken to guard them from the defilement of contact with the world. Yet their national annals, written by their own historians and prophets, contain an almost unbroken record of deliberate disobedience, of persistent and willful disregard of known commands, and of determined rebellion against divine authority, until they were cast out of the land. When Christ came, an aged Simeon and Anna waited for the consolation of Israel, but with hardly an exception the people had wholly departed from God. So the fourth trial ended in utter disaster and ruin.

The dispensation of our Lord's personal ministry followed. The result of the new experiment may be described in the words, "He was in the world, and the world was made by Him, and the world knew Him not. He came unto His own, and His own received Him not" (John 1:9–10). He performed the most mighty and the most convincing miracles almost without number; He spoke as never man did to thousands, and tens of thousands, but He won only a few followers, principally among the poor and illiterate and debased; and when He was nailed to the cross a mocking inscription was placed above His head in Hebrew, Greek, and Latin, the language of religion, the language of culture, and the language of power. All that Jew, Greek and Roman did for God's dear Son was to give Him a manger for a cradle, an instrument of torture on which to die, and a borrowed tomb to hold His mangled body. "He is despised and rejected of men" (Isa 53:3). So the fifth trial ended in utter disaster and ruin.

This brings us to the dispensation of the Spirit, so called because the Holy Spirit has come to bear witness to Christ's ascension, to reprove the world, to help believers as their abiding Comforter, to baptize all true saints into one body, of which our exalted Lord is the head. But so far as salvation is concerned, it is no more the dispensation of the Spirit than any former age, for every child of man who has been redeemed since Adam's day, has been saved by the Spirit through faith. Human nature and human need are precisely the same they have been from the fall of our first parents to this present time. It is clearly, therefore, not a question of the competency of the Spirit to save all men, nor of the adaptation of the Gospel to all men, but of the divine purpose as revealed in the inspired Scriptures.

If anyone can show a line in these Scriptures from the first of Genesis to the last of Revelation, which promises the conversion of the world by the agencies now employed, it becometh premillennialists to retire at once into silence and into seclusion from the field of controversy. Many a prominent preacher and professor boldly asserts that this dispensation of the Spirit has been appointed to bring the whole world to Christ. He is challenged to make good the assertion by the living word of God. "Let him now speak, or else hereafter forever hold his peace." Even he will admit that if such is the purpose of God, it has been terribly defeated for more than eighteen hundred and fifty years; if such was the design of the dispensation, it has miserably failed.

In the first place, although Christianity for the first three hundred years of our era rolled like a wave of blessing across the known and habitable globe, scarcely a trace of it is left where it was originally victorious. Churches by hundreds and thousands throughout Southern Europe, Northern Africa and Western Asia, were planted by the hands of the apostles or their immediate successors, and enriched with the blood of martyrs; but they have entirely disappeared from the face of the earth. The ground they occupied is as barren as heathenism. Remember that this occurred in the dispensation of the Spirit, as did the utter corruption of the church, culminating under Constantine, and spreading over Christendom like a black cloud, that for more than a thousand years was broken here and there by only a single ray of light.

In the second place, the Reformation was speedily followed by ratio-
nalism, and the country that gave birth to the former is now the home
of the latter. Within an incredibly short period after Luther's departure,
Jesus could have said to the most of Protestantism, as He said to the
church at Sardis, "I know thy works, that thou hast a name, that thou
livest, and art dead" (Rev 3:1). It took three hundred years to arouse the
cold, formal, lifeless mass to any sense of obligation to carry the gospel to
the perishing millions of our race, and although the century now closing
has been signalized by an enormous expenditure of money and of the
lives of men on the foreign field, and although, blessed be God, about
3,000,000 have professed the Christian faith, there are 200,000,000 more
to be converted than at the beginning of the century. The church in
heathen lands does not begin to keep pace with the natural increase by
birth of the Pagan and Mohammedan population. The Rev. James John-
ston, a devoted English missionary, tells us that "the actual increase of
the population is much more than the 200,000,000;" and "we rejoice in
the work accomplished by modern Christian missions, while we mourn
over the sad fact that the increase of the heathen is numerically *more
than seventy times* greater than that of the converts during the century
of missions." Nay, worse still; "the great heathen and Mohammedan
systems of religion are not only increasing their adherents by the ordinary
birthrate, but are yearly making far more converts than our Christian
missions."

In the third place, the outlook at home is not much more encouraging.
The bright-eyed optimists boast that there are 12,000,000 of Protestant
church members. Granted, but there are 50,000,000 more souls to be
converted than when the Constitution of the United States was adopted.
Their figures perplex a plain man who is not good in mathematics, when
he knows upon undoubted authority that not one in ten, at least of
our city people, can be induced to listen to the preaching of the gospel.
In New York City, for example, with its 1,500,000 inhabitants, only
85,000 were found on a fair day in its various places of worship; and if
every seat in every church, chapel, hall and other preaching station was
occupied every Sunday, there would still be 1,250,000 persons who could
not hear the gospel if they so desired. An item which has just appeared

in a sunny New York religious paper tells the story. It is as follows: "Churches and population below Fourteenth street: 1850, 36 churches, 400,000 population; 1890, 24 churches, 600,000 population." London with a population of 6,000,000, the most thoroughly evangelized city of the world, with the ablest preachers and the largest charities, furnishes church accommodations for only 1,500,000; and very few of its houses of worship are half filled. Let anyone read Gen. Booth's "In Darkest England," and see what is the dreadful condition of things in the heart of Christendom. A similar proportion of the neglected and of non-church goers is found in all of our principal cities.

In the fourth place, our leading professors in college and theological seminary, at least the professors who have the ear of the public and are most admired and applauded, seem to be determined to destroy the foundation of faith in the authority and certainty of God's word. A powerfully written article which recently appeared in a Chicago secular newspaper, well presents the case:

> "The sum of all is that the Bible is 'a fallible book,' consist-
> ing of 'idyls, myths, poems, fiction, dreams, predictions,
> histories, novels, morals and theology,' full of 'human in-
> ventions and imperfections,' with traces of the divine in
> it, but, of itself, 'no absolute criterion of faith, morals or
> worship.' ... The impertinent assault of Dr. Schaff, Profes-
> sor Briggs' colleague, upon the Westminster Confession,
> sent a shock through all the churches two years ago....
> And, more recently, the so-called 'American Institute of
> Sacred Literature,' with Professors Briggs and Harper in
> the lead, teaching that the authority of Jesus Christ and
> His apostles amounts to nothing in questions of 'higher
> criticism,' since they did not profess to be critics, and
> had another mission—and teaching this in Chicago and
> Boston under the auspices of the Young Men's Christian
> Association—has given intensity to the situation.... This
> is not a Presbyterian, or a Baptist, or a Congregational

fight. It is an open apostasy in the bosom of professing Christendom. Not one solitary Assembly or Association or Conference has taken action on the subject. The poison is deep in the veins of the denominations. An eminent Professor in Berlin, another in Neuchatel, another in Vienna, and another in Dorpat have recently written that 'nothing now can stay the tide of defection from the faith which is rising in the bosom of Christendom,' and 'the church can only expect the divine judgments her sins have provoked.' 'A higher critic, enthroned above all earthly critics, will avenge the wrongs done to His own Word and to Himself.'"

The sudden outburst of infidelity among able, and learned, and eloquent and influential Professors, who are connected with schools for the training of young men, soon to become pastors, is one of the most significant signs of the times. Besides Professor Briggs and Professor Harper with their destructive "Higher Criticism," borrowed of course from the Germans, we have Professor Schurman in the Congregational church, Professor Allen in the Episcopal, Professor Workman in the Methodist, publishing statements about the Bible that might make Mr. Ingersoll blush. On the other side of the Atlantic we have Professor Dods, Professor Drummond, Professor Smyth, Professor Davidson assailing the inspiration of God's word, denying the fall of man, the atonement of Christ, and every essential truth. Professor Momerie of the theological department in King's College is just out in a book in which he tells us that the inspiration of the Scripture does not differ in quality from that of Shakespeare or Newton.

Let the following suffice to show his teachings that are gladly accepted by many theological Professors of our day:

> "Between the covers of this little volume (the Bible) we find opinions as diverse and contradictory as have ever existed in the world. And in particular we can trace it

in the development of the idea of God from barbarism up to Hegel.... The modern priest talks about miracles—Gadarene pigs, and what not—as he might have done at a time when natural laws had never been heard of, when everyone believed, not in the uniformity, but in the irregularity of Nature.... He speaks about inspiration and revelation, as if he did not know that much of the teaching of the Bible had been equaled, and even surpassed, in other sacred literatures, and that some of the sayings of Christ Himself—including even the golden rule—had been anticipated by 'pagans' hundreds of years before the Christian era.... There is a practically infinite difference between the God of the patriarchs, who is always repenting, and the God of the apostles.... It is strange that persons who have read the 25th chapter of Matthew should still believe in the doctrine of Justification by Faith."

The Rev. Minot J. Savage D.D., a Unitarian preacher of Boston, no doubt tells the truth in a recently published discourse, when he says:

"There are any number of places in America where there would be Unitarian churches within three months, were it not for the fact that the nominally orthodox ministers of those places have taken the wind completely out of the Unitarian sails. The people say, 'What is the use of a Unitarian Church? Our minister is as broad as yours; he no longer preaches an infallible Bible, or hell, or the Trinity.'"

He is no doubt truthful also in the statement that a prominent minister, orthodox in name, declared to him he did not know one preacher in his large circle of acquaintance who now believes these doctrines. Can anyone fail to see that there has been a departure from the Bible, as wide as infidelity, by numbers who give instruction from the pulpit?

In the fifth place, the pew is in a still more deplorable condition, if this were possible. The atmosphere is laden with the malaria of skepticism, as it is said to be charged with the microbes of deadly disease, and the members of the church inhale it, like others. The germs of unbelief cling to nearly all of our current literature, being found not only in the works of scientists, who are almost to a man earnest agnostics or avowed atheists, but also in magazines, newspapers, good-for-nothing novels, and even in volumes of popular sermons. *The British Weekly*, which is anything but a pessimistic periodical, declares it to be "a fact that the vast majority of the *younger* men, who are providing the best journalism of the day, are unbelievers. They do not even accept the idea of a GOD."

It is not surprising, therefore, that professing Christians who read much are carried away from the truth. It is one of the many evidences of the supernatural origin of the Scriptures that they come into sharp conflict with human nature, and if human nature is given a chance, even the human nature of a professing Christian, it will take sides every time against God and His word. This is the secret of the excessive popularity of such religious writers as Professor Drummond. "He adapts Christianity to its present environment," as one of his admirers has said, and throws down the reins upon the neck of man's natural desires and self-suffi- ciency. The educational process of substituting human opinion for the authority of the inspired writings has gone to such extent, that a vast majority of those who have confessed the name of Christ are almost as ignorant of the Bible, as if no such book had been written. They prefer to travel on His day for business or pleasure, or if they stay at home, their minds are stuffed with the crime and gossip, the scandal and politics of the Sunday newspaper before they observe the empty form of public worship. The most startling thing about it is the utter deadness of conscience to any claim of God. Numbers of them are living in open and notorious sin, and yet their names are enrolled on the church registers, and they come to the Lord's table under the fatal delusion that they are Christians. Scarcely a day passes without the mention in the newspapers or the names even of ministers of the gospel in connection with licentiousness; and so numerous are defaulters and thieves who are

Sunday School teachers and church officers, they have ceased to excite surprise.

Even among the others who maintain a decent outward deportment, how few manifest any real spiritual life! What a mere handful of any considerable congregation in the land can be found in the prayer-meeting, or Sunday-school, or kneeling in family worship, or speaking a word for Christ, so far as can be ascertained! The most of those who appear before the world as the representatives of the Lord Jesus, attend the theatre, or send their children to the dancing school, or whirl in the lustful waltz, or carry on gambling in their own houses under the name of progressive euchre, or they are tricky in trade, or covetous and stingy, or mean and untruthful, ungodly in their amusements, conversation, fashions, habits, maxims, principles, purposes, and reading, no one being able to discover the faintest line of separation between them and the world. Dear Dr. Bonor truly said, "I look for the church, and find it in the world; I look for the world, and find it in the church." A few years ago, a somewhat notorious Catholic-Episcopal or Episcopal-Catholic clergyman of New York city caused quite a hubbub by declaring that Protestantism is a failure. But if judged by the standard of doctrine and duty revealed in the New Testament, the man was right. Or, if it is expected to convert the world, he was right. In this respect, both Protestantism and Popery are wretched failures. The world has converted them.

In the sixth place, society is leprous all over. Upon this subject it is enough perhaps, to quote Elizabeth Stuart Phelps, one of the purest and most popular of our writers:

> "A prominent literary man, himself used to the world and the ways thereof, urged earnestly upon the author [of] the publication of this paper, saying, 'In my humble opinion, the ideal of propriety held by what is called society, has absolutely no relation to the moral sense. To take a point; when I see the ease, nay, the eagerness with which our young girls attend and seem to prefer those plays where the ballet is enough to make any gentleman uncomfort-

able, I am confused. What does it mean?' ... Our stage
exhibits moral monstrosity to the edge of abomination ...
while the fathers of our girls pay two dollars and a half a
seat for the privilege of exposing their daughters to sights
which ought to be suppressed under the law prohibiting
the exhibition of obscene pictures."

Of course her noble indignation will be sneered at as prudery, as her
denunciations of the dance will be; and the young girls will continue to
swarm to the obscene exhibitions of the theatre, and to be clasped in the
embrace of men.

"Any fashion which gives to a *roue*[1] the right to clasp a
pure woman in his arms, and hold her for the length of
an intoxicating piece of music, is below moral defense. I
firmly believe that the time will come when our present
license in this respect will be regarded as we now regard the
practices attending the worship of Aphrodite. It might be
said that nautch dance [a dance performed by prostitutes]
is modesty beside our waltz.... One need not be a fanatic
in the temperance movement to discern one cause for the
decrease of modesty in the increase of drinking habits
among a certain class of our ladies. 'Certainly,' testifies
the first young man I happen to ask, himself a person of
so-called good morals; 'certainly I have often danced with
young ladies who were intoxicated. It is not an uncom-
mon thing to meet them "too far gone" to converse.' If the
delicacy of a sober girl cannot protect her from the taint
in the social atmosphere, what is to be expected from the
modesty of a drunken one? ... In the old times a modest

---

1. A roue (or roué) is a French word describing a man dedicated to
sensual pleasure.

wife hardly conversed with her own husband as young
women do today with young men of their acquaintance....
It is a fact, gloss it anyhow as we may, that decent women
have never dressed so indecently in our country and century as they do in fashionable life today."

Perhaps it is well to add the opening of last New Year's address by Dr.
Talmage, the most popular preacher in America, and the most hopeful
optimist, who always looks on the "bright side," and who calls upon the
church for a forward movement.

"That there is need for such a religious movement is evident from the fact that never since our world was swung
out among the planets has there been such an organized
and determined effort to overthrow righteousness, and
make the ten commandments obsolete and the whole
Bible a derision. Meanwhile alcoholism is taking down its
victims by the hundreds of thousands, and the political
parties get down on their knees practically saying, 'O thou
Rum Jug, we bow down before thee. Give us the offices,
city, state and national. Oh, give us the offices and we
will worship thee forever and ever, Amen.' The Christian
Sabbath, meanwhile, appointed for physical, mental and
spiritual rest, is being secularized and abolished. As if the
bad publishing houses of our own country had exhausted
their literary filth, the French and Russian sewers have
been invited to pour their scurrility and moral slush into
the trough, where our American swine are now wallow-
ing. Meanwhile, there are enough marts of infamy in all
our city, open and unmolested of the law, to invoke the
Omnipotent wrath, which buried Sodom under a deluge of brimstone. The pandemoniac world, I think, has
massed its troops, and they are this moment playing their
batteries upon family circles, church circles, social circles

and national circles. Apollyon is in the saddle and, riding
at the head of his myrmidons, would capture this world
for darkness and woe."

In the seventh place, neither the government of the United States nor
of any other nation in Christendom, possesses the elements of stability.
The vile immoralities of men in public life, both in Great Britain and in
America, to say nothing of the determined and desperate socialism per-
vading the working classes, and the rapid increase of crime and drunkenness and licentiousness and vice in every form are surely rotting away
the foundations on which alone empires and republics stand. A friend,
who has carefully looked over the columns of a daily city newspaper for
a single month of the year 1891, reports that he read accounts of 404
murders and 586 other crimes, such as adultery, burglary, robbery and
rape, some of which were worse than brutal, for they were devilish. Add
to this the statistics brought out in a paper read before the Young Men's
Christian Association Convention of Illinois, in 1890, telling us "that
we have about 7,000,000 of young men between eighteen and thirty, and
that 6,000,000 of these never attend a church; that only about 350,000
are members of any church; while there are over 700,000 young men
between those ages in our public prisons at some time during each year."

In this country for the past fifteen years the most earnest and persistent
efforts have been made by good men, and by organized bands of women,
to put an end to the drink traffic, and to arrest the frightful evils of
intemperance. How far these efforts have succeeded may be learned from
the following table just received directly from the Revenue Office in
Washington City.

- Under the head, "Distilled Spirits Consumed," it appears
  that in 1875 there were 66,120,588 gallons used; in 1890,
  87,829,562 gallons.

- Under the head, "Wine Consumed," in 1875 there were
  19,991,330 gallons; in 1889, these had increased to 34,144,477
  gallons.

- Under the head, "Malt Liquors Consumed," the people in
  1875 drank 294,953,157 gallons; and in 1890 they swallowed
  856,792,335 gallons.

When we add to these figures the appalling fact that there is an annual
expenditure in this so-called Christian land of $900,000,000 for liquor,
and $600,000,000 for tobacco, while the paltry sum of $5,500,000 is
given to Home and Foreign Missions, it is evident that the millennium
has not yet dawned, but it is growing darker every day.

Senator Ingalls, of Kansas, perhaps the keenest intellect in the United
States Senate, whatever may be thought of him as a man or politician,
recently delivered before the Senate a carefully prepared oration, which
opened as follows:

> "Mr. President, two portentous perils threaten the safety,
> if they do not endanger the existence, of the republic.
> The first of these is ignorant, debased, degraded, spurious,
> and sophisticated suffrage, contaminated by the sewage
> of decaying nations; suffrage intimidated and suppressed
> in the South; suffrage impure and corrupt, apathetic and
> indifferent, in the great cities of the North; so that it is
> doubtful whether there has been for half a century a pres-
> idential election in this country that expressed the delib-
> erate and intelligent judgment of the whole body of the
> American people. The second evil Mr. President, to which
> I adverted as threatening the safety, if it does not endanger
> the existence, of the republic, is the tyranny of combined,
> concentrated, centralized, and incorporated capital. [He
> then shows that of the enormous wealth of the country,
> $65,000,000,000, considerably more than one-half is in
> the hands of 31,100 persons.] Mr. President, it is the most
> appalling statement that ever fell upon mortal ears. It is,
> so far as the results of democracy as a social and political
> experiment are concerned the most terrible commentary
> that ever was recorded in the book of time—and Nero fid-

dles while Rome burns. It is thrown off with a laugh and a sneer, 'as the froth upon the beer' of our political and social system.... Nor is this all, Mr. President; the hostility between the employers and the employed in this country is becoming vindictive and permanently malevolent. Labor and capital are in two hostile camps today. Lockouts and strikes and labor difficulties have become practically the normal condition of our system, and it is estimated that during the year that has just closed, in consequence of these disorders, in consequence of this hostility and this warfare, the actual loss to the country has not been less than $300,000,000."

The saddest feature about it all is the fact that the laboring men, or wage-workers, or breadwinners, as they are foolishly called, hate the church with the bitterest hatred. They regard it as part of the fashionable and wealthy society which, they complain, deprives them of their rights. Upon this large and important class of the community, the Protestant church, at least, has almost entirely lost its hold. Not one in ten thousand of them ever goes near a building in which religions services are observed, and it must be confessed, that the appearance of the congregation, and the intellectual preaching, on the inside are not calculated to draw them. When we find our great scientific authorities announcing that there is no God, and our leading professors declaring that the Bible is not true, and our most popular preachers proclaiming that there is no future punishment, even one who is not the son of a prophet can safely predict that the sources of morality will soon be dried, and the barriers to universal lawlessness speedily removed. No wonder that at the close of the present age the vial of divine wrath is poured out upon the sea; "and it became as the blood of a dead man" (Rev 16:3).

Only a glance has been given to some of the difficulties and evils that lie upon the very surface of things. Very much more could have been truthfully written under each of the topics here presented; but perhaps enough has been said to convince any fair-minded reader of the utter failure of man under the best circumstances. It is distasteful, however, to most persons to face unpleasant facts, and hence the actual facts, now presented in the mildest manner, will be scouted,[2] just as the few who predicted the late civil war, arguing from the inevitable logic of current events and from the unavoidable relation of cause to effect, were ridiculed as cranks and pessimists. So the mass of the people and the preachers will continue to laugh, claiming that the church has never been in so flourishing a condition, declaring that the world is becoming better every day, until the storm of God's wrath shall burst upon them, as the rain of fire and brimstone swept the cities of the plain.

There is an absolute necessity for the personal coming of the Lord Jesus Christ to save an apostate church and a godless, undone world. Never has any former age terminated in more complete disaster and ruin than that which confronts the professing Christian body in the dispensation of the Spirit. Nay, in proportion to the height of privilege to which the gospel has exalted those who have heard its glad tidings, will be the depth of their fall; and the ruin of the house, built not upon the impregnable rock of Scripture but upon the sand, shall be great. Even at the end of the millennial period, the seventh dispensation, there will be a final attempt of the liberated Satan and the confederated nations to destroy the authority of Jehovah. It will be amply demonstrated to angels and men and demons that, however cultivated and wherever placed, "the mind of the flesh is enmity against God" (Rom 8:7).

> The day of the Lord it cometh,
> It cometh like a thief in the night,
> It comes when the world is dreaming
> Of safety and of peace and light;
> It cometh, the day of sackcloth,
> With darkness, and storm, and tire,
> The day of the Great Avenger,
> The day of the burning ire.

---

2. In this context, scouted means to be mocked.

The day of the Lord it cometh,
When the virgins are all asleep,
And the drunken world is lying
In a slumber yet more deep;
Like a sudden lurch of the vessel,
By night on the sunken rock.
All earth in a moment reeleth,
And goeth down with the shock.

The flash of the sword of havoc
Foretelleth the day of blood,
Revealing the Judge's progress,
The downward march of God;
The fire which no mortal kindles,
Quick seizes the quaking earth,
And labors the groaning creation
In the pangs of its second birth.

Then the day of the evil endeth.
And the righteous reign comes in,
Like a cloud of sorrow evanish,
The ages of human sin;
The light of the morning gleameth
Adown, without cloud or gloom,
In chains lies the ruler of darkness,
And the Prince of Light has come!

12

A Practical Hope

Beyond question the doctrine of our Lord's second coming is the commanding motive of the New Testament. Not even the love of Christ is so frequently mentioned as an incentive. It is connected by the Holy Ghost with every doctrine and duty, with every precept and practice of Christian faith and conduct. It arms admonitions, it points appeals, it strengthens arguments, it enforces commands, it intensifies entreaties, it arouses courage, it rebukes fear, it quickens affection, it kindles hope, it inflames zeal, it separates from the world, it consecrates to God, it dries tears, it conquers death. No one will deny that it is found everywhere through gospels and epistles, although many will affirm that the passages containing it do not mean what they declare.

A dear old ex-pastor of Brooklyn, celebrated for the number of his charming contributions to religious periodicals, and still more noted for his enormous egotism, has recently informed the public that one hundred printed texts on the second advent have no more to do with the coming of the Lord than with the McKinley tariff bill. This shows, not only the density of the dear old Doctor's ignorance, but the weakness of the silly subterfuge by which some of the beloved postmillennial brethren seek to evade the truth concerning our Saviour's personal return. Every one of the one hundred texts touches directly upon that personal return, as do the texts now presented in the form of a Second Advent Alphabet, and these by no means exhaust the subject.

ABIDING in Christ. "And now, little children, abide in Him; that when He shall appear, we may have confidence, and not be ashamed before Him at His coming" (1 John 2:28).

BROTHERLY LOVE. "The Lord make you to increase and abound in love one toward another, and toward all men, even as we do toward you; to the end He may establish your hearts unblameable in holiness before God, even our Father, at the coming of our Lord Jesus Christ with all His saints" (1 Thess 3:12–13).

CONSOLATION. "I would not have you to be ignorant, brethren, concerning them which are asleep, that ye sorrow not, even as others which have no hope. For if we believe that Jesus died and rose again, even so them also which sleep in Jesus will God bring with Him" (1 Thess 4:13–14).

DEADNESS TO SIN. "When Christ, who is our life, shall appear, then shall ye also appear with Him in glory. Mortify therefore your members which are upon the earth" (Col 3:4–5).

ENDURANCE. "Behold, I come quickly: hold that fast which thou hast, that no man take thy crown" (Rev 3:11). "Whosoever, therefore, shall be ashamed of me and of my words in this adulterous and sinful generation, of him, shall the Son of man be ashamed, when He cometh in the glory of His father with the holy angels" (Mark 8:38).

FAITHFULNESS. "A certain nobleman went into a far country to receive for himself a kingdom, and to return. And he called his ten servants, and delivered them ten pounds, and said unto them, Occupy until I come" (Luke 19:12–13).

GODLINESS. "The day of the Lord will come as a thief in the night.... Seeing then that all these things shall he dissolved, what manner of persons ought ye to be in all holy conversation and godliness, looking for and hasting the coming of the day of God" (2 Pet 3:10–12).

HEAVENLY-MINDEDNESS. "Our citizenship is in heaven; from whence also we look for the Saviour, the Lord Jesus Christ" (Phil 3:20). "Beloved, now are we the sons of God; and it doth not yet appear what we shall be; but we know that when He shall appear, we shall be like Him, for we shall see Him as He is. And every man that hath this hope in Him purifieth himself, even as He is pure" (1 John 3:2–3).

INSTATANEOUS. "As the lightning cometh out of the east, and shineth even unto the west; so also shall the coming of the Son of Man be" (Matt 24:27).

JUDGMENT. "Behold, the Lord cometh with ten thousands of His saints, to execute judgment upon all" (Jude 14–15). "When the Son of Man shall come in His glory, and all the holy angels with Him, then shall He sit upon the throne of His glory, and before Him shall be gathered all nations" (Matt 25:31–32).

KEEPING THE GARMENTS. "Behold, I come as a thief. Blessed is He that watcheth, and keepeth his garments, lest he walk naked, and they see his shame" (Rev 16:15).

LORD'S SUPPER. "As oft as ye eat this bread, and drink this cup, ye do shew the Lord's death till He come" (1 Cor 11:26). "If I go and prepare a place for you, I will come again, and receive you unto myself" (John 14:3). "Unto them that look for Him shall He appear a second time, without sin unto salvation" (Heb 9:28).

MODERATION. "Let your moderation be known unto all men. The Lord is at hand" (Phil 4:5). "Therefore judge nothing before the time, until the Lord come" (1 Cor 4:5).

NEARNESS. "Yet a little while and He that shall come will come, and will not tarry" (Heb 10:37). Stablish your hearts: for the coming of the Lord draweth nigh" (James 5:8).

OBEDIENCE. "The Lord Jesus shall be revealed from heaven with His mighty angels, in flaming fire, taking vengeance on them that know not God, and that obey not the gospel of our Lord Jesus Christ" (2 Thess 1:7–8).

PATIENCE. "Be patient, therefore, brethren unto the coming of the Lord" (James 5:7). "The Lord direct your hearts into the love of God, and into the patient waiting for Christ" (2 Thess 3:5).

QUICKLY. "Behold, I come quickly" (Rev 22:7). "He which testifieth these things saith, surely I come quickly; Amen. Even so, come. Lord Jesus" (Rev 22:20).

REWARD. "The Son of Man shall come in the glory of His Father with His angels; and then He shall reward every man according to his works" (Matt 16:27). "Behold, I come quickly; and my reward is with me, to give every man as his work shall be" (Rev 22:12).

SANCTIFICATION. "The God of peace Himself sanctify you wholly; and may your spirit and soul and body be preserved entire, without blame, at the coming of our Lord Jesus Christ" (1 Thess 5:23, Revised Version).

TRIALS. "That the trial of your faith, being much more precious than of gold that perisheth, though it be tried with fire, might be found unto praise and honor and glory at the appearing of Jesus Christ" (1 Pet 1:7).

UNREBUKABLE. "I give thee charge in the sight of God, who quickeneth all things, and of Christ Jesus, who before Pontius Pilate witnessed a good confession; that thou keep this commandment without spot, unrebukable, until the appearing of our Lord Jesus Christ" (1 Tim 6:13–14).

VIGILANCE. "Let your loins be girded about, and your lights burning; and ye yourselves like unto men that wait for the Lord" (Luke 12:35). "Watch ye therefore; for ye know not when the Master of the house cometh, at even, or at midnight, or at the cockcrowing, or in the morning: lest coming suddenly He find you sleeping. And what I say unto you I say unto all, Watch" (Mark 13:35–37).

WAITING. "Ye turned to God from idols, to serve the living and true God, and to wait for His Son from Heaven, whom He raised from the dead, Jesus who delivered us from the wrath to come" (1 Thess 1:9–10). "Ye come behind in no gift; waiting for the coming of our Lord Jesus Christ" (1 Cor 1:7).

'XCELLENT. "That ye may approve things that are excellent; that ye may be sincere and without offence until the day of Christ" (Phil 1:9–10).

YEARNING. "Looking for [*prosdekomai*, expecting, waiting for] that blessed hope, and appearing of the glory of our great God and Saviour Jesus Christ" (Titus 2:13). "Even we ourselves groan within ourselves, waiting for the adoption, the redemption of our body" (Rom 8:23). "Christ the firstfruits; afterward they that are Christ's at His coming" (1 Cor 15:23).

ZEAL. "I have fought a good fight, I have finished my course, I have kept the faith; henceforth there is laid up for me a crown of righteousness, which the Lord, the righteous Judge, will give me at that day; and not to me only, but unto all them also that love His appearing" (2 Tim

4:7–8). "Blessed are those servants whom the Lord, when He cometh, shall find watching" (Luke 12:37). "That which ye have already, hold fast till I come" (Rev 2:25). "Behold I come quickly; hold that fast which thou hast, that no man take thy crown" (Rev 3:11).

Anyone can easily see that if the doctrine is practically received, it must become a practical power in the life. For example, the premillennialist reads the words of his Lord, "This gospel of the kingdom shall be preached in all the world for a witness unto all nations; and then shall the end come" (Matt 24:14); and animated by the hope of hastening the end, and the coming of the King, and the overthrow of the world rulers of this darkness, he joyfully embarks in foreign missionary enterprises. Scores and hundreds of faithful ambassadors for Christ in heathen lands testify that they caught a mighty and abiding impulse to labor on, in the face of sore discouragements, when they embraced the hope of His coming as their governing principle.

J. Hudson Taylor, at the head of the China Inland Mission, and his more than 300 devoted missionaries, are all earnest premillennialists. Dr. H. Grattan Guinness, founder of the Congo Mission, who annually sends a number of his premillennial students to the heathen world, is an earnest premillennialist. Rev John Wilkinson, with singular self-denial conducting missions among the Jews of Europe, and all his assistants, are earnest premillennialists. Reginald Radcliffe, Esq., travelling for years from place to place in the interests of foreign missions, is an earnest premillennialist. George Muller, a missionary nearly ninety years of age, and supporting a number of premillennial missionaries, is an earnest premillennialist. Dr. A. T. Pierson, editor of the best missionary review ever printed, who has done more than any other man in America to arouse the churches from their guilty indifference to the perishing millions of earth, is an earnest premillennialist. Dr. A. J. Gordon, at the head of the training school for foreign missions among the Baptists, is an earnest premillennialist. W. E. Blackstone, Esq., at the head of a training school for foreign missions among the Methodists, is an earnest premillennialist. Rev. C. I. Scofield, at the head of a training school for foreign missions among the Congregationalists, is an earnest premillennialist. The young men and women who went from Kansas to the Soudan, glad to lay down their lives for Jesus, were all earnest premillennialists. So easy is it to cut the nerve of the stale slander that faith in the premillennial coming of the Lord cuts the nerve of missionary effort.

In Christian lands, as they are called, Christian in profession and heathen in practice, the same stimulating effect of the truth is seen in the lives of Evangelists all of whom in Great Britain, perhaps without exception, and all of whom in the United States, with only one exception that is known, are earnest premillennialists. The secret of their untiring activity and fervor was happily expressed by poor Henry Ward Beecher, when he described them as men engaged in saving as many as possible from a wrecked and sinking ship. They believe that "the time is short" (1 Cor 7:29), or as the Greek word implies, that the time for furling in sail has come; and they are anxious to take with them as many as they can lay hands upon into the harbor of eternal rest.

To the believer engaged in ordinary occupations, the hope of the Lord's return comes as a divine power to separate him from the world. He is like a young Christian, who, after his conversion to the premillennial faith, was asked by a friend to accompany him to a theatre. "No," was the reply; "the Lord may come tonight, and I do not wish him to find me in a place where He Himself would not be welcome." It is impossible for a man who is walking in the golden beams of that hope to live like the ungodly around him. He knows that he is a stranger and pilgrim amid these vanishing scenes, and he is careful not to fasten his tent pins too deep in the earth. His aims and aspirations, his purposes and pursuits, his tastes and tendencies are all different from the ambitions, and customs, and objects of the social and political circles through which he moves as a citizen of another country. Dr. David Brown bears the following true testimony to the premillennial doctrine:

> "It is a school of scripture interpretation: It impinges
> upon and effects some of the most commanding points
> of the Christian faith; and, when suffered to work its
> unimpeded way, it stops not till it has pervaded with its
> own genius the entire system of one's theology, and the

whole tone of his spiritual character, constructing, I had almost said, a world of its own; so that, holding the same faith, and cherishing the same fundamental hopes as other Christians, he yet sees things through a medium of his own, and finds everything instinct with the life which this doctrine has generated within him."

Especially do these remarks apply to the view which the premillennialist takes of death. He hopes that he will not die at all, for he knows that "we shall not all sleep" (1 Cor 15:51). He would not be "unclothed, but clothed upon that mortality might be swallowed up of life" (2 Cor 5:4); and he desires to be among those of whom it is written, "we which are alive and remain, shall be caught up together with them in the clouds, to meet the Lord in the air" (1 Thess 4:17). Hence, he is amazed to hear Christians say that the coming of the Lord and death are one and the same, or that there is no difference between them. No difference! One is all gladness, and the other is all sadness. One is all glory, and the other is all gloom. One is all morning, and the other is all midnight. Out upon the base suggestion! It makes one indignant to hear that any dare put the hateful and loathsome monster death, that with ruffian violence has torn away our darlings, that with black wing, as of a cyclone, has darkened our homes, in the place of the sweet and most precious coming of our Lord, which will prevent death. The premillennialist reads with joy that death is to be cast into the lake of fire at the judgment of the Great White Throne (Rev 20:14).

> "Waiting we stand,
> And watching till our Saviour shall appear,
> Joyful to cry, as eastern skies grow clear,
> 'The Lord's at hand!'

But now the night
Presses around us, sullenly and chill;
Pain, doubt, and sorrow seem to have their will:
Lord, send the light!

One after one,
Thou hast called up our loved ones from our sight;
For them we know that there is no more night
But we are a lone.

Weary we wait,
Lifting our heavy eyes, bedimmed with tears,
To skies where yet no trace of dawn appears—
Lord, it is late!

But yet thy word
Saith, with sweet prophecy that cannot fail,
That light o'er darkness shall at length prevail—
We trust thee Lord!

O Morning Star
Of heavenly promise! light our darkened way,
Till the first beams of the expected day
Shine from afar.

So will we take
Fresh hope and courage to our fainting hearts,
And patient wait, though every joy departs,
'Till the day break.'"

13

Witnesses to the Hope

It is needless, perhaps, to affirm that the early Christians were premillennialists. That is, they looked for the speedy personal return of the Lord Jesus, and did not dream of a spiritual millennium, or the conversion of the world by the church. This is freely admitted by Dr. Charles Hodge, Mr. Albert Barnes, Prof. Hackett and all other postmillennial expositors without exception, so far as known. All no doubt would heartily agree with the remarks of Mr. Barnes on the words *to wait for His Son from Heaven* (1 Thess 1:10).

> "It is clear from this and from other parts of these two epistles, that the return of the Lord Jesus to this world was a prominent subject of the preaching of Paul at Thessalonica. In the passage before us, he says that the return of the Son of God from heaven was an important point which had been insisted on when he was there; and that their conduct, as borne witness to by all, had shown with what power it had seized upon them, and what a practical influence it had exerted in their lives.... It is eminently adapted to comfort the hearts of true Christians in the sorrows, bereavements, and sicknesses of life (John 14:1–3; Acts 1:11; 1 Thess 4:13–18; 2 Pet 3:8–9); to lead us to watchfulness and to an earnest inquiry into the question whether we are prepared to meet Him (Matt 24:37–44; 25:13); to make us dead to the world, and to lead us to act as becomes the children of light (1 Thess

5:5–9); to awaken and arouse impenitent and careless sin-
ners (1 Thess 5:2–3; 2 Pet 3:3–7), and to excite Christians to self-denying efforts to spread the gospel in distant
lands, as was the case at Thessalonica. Every doctrine of
the gospel is adapted to produce some happy practical
effects in mankind, but there are few that are more full of
elevated and holy influences than that which teaches that
the Lord Jesus will return to the earth, and which leads
the soul to wait for his appearing."

If the objection is raised that Mr. Barnes, and the other commentators
named, were themselves postmillennialists, the answer is at hand. The
testimony of an unwilling witness is always and properly considered
more conclusive than the testimony of a witness, whose prejudices or
interests incline him to the evidence he gives. If these gentleman had
found any way to escape the conclusion that the early Christians stood
in an attitude of expecting the personal coming of Christ, they would
certainly have availed themselves most gladly of an opportunity, at least,
to keep silent upon the subject. We have nothing to do with their opin-
ions, but only with their testimony concerning the universal belief of the
first disciples.

Thus we are not compelled to accept the rationalistic tendencies of
Prof. Harnack, although forced to bow to his testimony as a historian,
because he is everywhere recognized as the ablest patristic scholar now
living. Evidently he is not in sympathy with the truth of our Lord's
premillennial coming, but he is obliged as an honest witness to place
upon record what he has discovered by a thorough search into the Christian literature of the first centuries. It is scarcely necessary to say that
millennium is a Latin word, and *chiliad* is a Greek word, both referring
to the *thousand* years when Satan shall be bound, when the righteous
dead shall be raised, and when shall be fulfilled the sweet benediction,
"Blessed and holy is he that hath part in the first resurrection; on such
the second death hath no power, but they shall be priests of God and of
Christ, and shall reign with Him a thousand years" (Rev 20:6).

> "In the history of Christianity three main forces are found
> to have acted as auxiliaries of the gospel. They have elicited
> the ardent enthusiasm of many whom the bare preaching
> of the gospel would never have made decided converts.
> These are (1) a belief in the speedy return of Christ and in
> His glorious reign on earth.... First in point of time came
> the faith in the nearness of Christ's second advent and
> the establishing of His reign of glory on the earth. Indeed
> it appears so early that it might be questioned whether
> it ought not to be regarded as an essential part of the
> Christian religion."

He then quotes from a number of men who labored with the apostles,
or were their immediate successors in the office of preaching the gospel,
all going to show that it may still be questioned whether the Lord's
personal and premillennial return to the earth may not be regarded as
an essential part of the Christian religion.

> "That a philosopher like Justin, with a bias towards a
> Hellenic construction of the Christian religion, should
> nevertheless have accepted its chiliastic elements, is the
> strongest proof that these enthusiastic expectations were
> inseparably bound up with the Christian faith down to
> the middle of the 2nd century. And another proof is
> found in the fact that even a speculative Jewish Christian
> like Cerinthus not only did not renounce the chiliastic
> hope, but pictured the future kingdom of Christ as a
> kingdom of sensual pleasures, of eating and drinking and
> marriage festivities.
>
> After the middle of the 2nd century these expectations
> were gradually thrust into the background. They would
> never have died out, however, had not circumstances al-

tered, and a new mental attitude been taken up. The spirit
of philosophical and theological speculation and of ethical
reflection, which began to spread through the churches, did not know what to make of the old hopes of the
future. So early as the year 170, a church party in Asia
Minor—the so-called Alogi—rejected the whole body of
apocalyptic writings and denounced the Apocalypse of
John as a book of fables. All the more powerful was the
reaction. In the so-called Montanistic controversy (AD
160–220), one of the principal issues involved was the
continuance of the chiliastic expectations in the churches.... After the Montanistic controversy, chiliastic views
were more and more discredited in the Greek Church;
they were, in fact, stigmatized as 'Jewish' and consequently 'heretical.' It was the Alexandrian theology that su-
perseded them; that is to say, Neoplatonic mysticism tri-
umphed over the early Christian hope of the future, first
among the 'cultured,' and then, when the theology of the
'cultured' had taken the faith of the 'uncultured' under its
protection, amongst the latter also."

Just so. The spirit of philosophical and theological speculation and
of ethical reflection, and Neoplatonic mysticism patronized by the cultured, are enough to kill all faith, not only in the coming of Christ, but
in Christ Himself. This is the trouble with the church of the present day,
and unless it gives up the folly, it will drift, as the church did after sur-
rendering the hope of the Lord's coming, into the dark ages. Philosophical and theological speculation, and ethical reflection, and Neoplatonic
mysticism and culture are choking the life out of the professing people
of God; and the devil stands by laughing.

"But the Western Church was also more conservative
than the Greek. Her theologians had, to begin with, little
turn for mystical speculation; their tendency was rather

to reduce the gospel to a system of morals. Now for the morality, chiliasm had a special significance as the one distinguishing feature of the gospel, and the only thing that gave a specifically Christian character to their system. This, however, holds good of the Western theologians only after the middle of the 3rd century. The earlier fathers, Irenaeus, Hippolytus, Tertullian, believed in chiliasm simply because it was a part of the tradition of the church, and because Marcion and the Gnostics would have nothing to do with it. Hippolytus, although an opponent to Montanism, was nevertheless a thoroughgoing millenarian. Tertullian aimed at a more spiritual conception of the millennial blessings than Papias had, but he still adhered, especially in the Montanistic period, to all the ancient anticipations. It is the same all through the 3rd and 4th centuries with those Latin theologians who escaped the influence of Greek speculation. Commodian, Victorinus Pattavensis, Lactantius and Sulpicius Severus, were all pronounced millenarians ... the clearest evidence that in the West millenarianism was still a point of 'orthodoxy' in the 4th century."

Prof. Harnack attributes the overthrow of the early faith to the great influence of Augustine, who at one time held it.

"But the signs of the times pointed to a different prospect. Without any miraculous interposition of God, not only was Christianity victorious on earth, but the church had attained a position of supremacy. The old Roman empire was tottering to its fall; the church stood fast, ready to step into the inheritance. It was not simply that the world-power, the enemy of Christ, had been vanquished; the fact as that it had gradually abdicated its political functions in favor of the church. [Alas! how true.] ... How

millenarianism nevertheless found its way, with the help
of apocalyptic mysticisms and Anabaptist influences, into
the churches of the Reformation, chiefly among the Reformed sects, but afterward, also in the Lutheran church,
how it became incorporated with Pietism, how in recent
time an exceeding mild type of 'academic' chiliasm *has
been developed from a belief in the verbal inspiration of
the Bible*, how finally new sects are springing up here and
there with apocalyptic and chiliastic expectations—these
are matters which cannot be entered upon here. But one
remark ought to be made in conclusion. A genuine and
living revival of chiliastic hopes is always a sign that the
church at large has become secularized to such a degree
that tender consciences can no longer feel sure of their
faith within her.... The claims of chiliasm are sufficiently met by the acknowledgment that in former times it
was, associated—to all appearance inseparably associated—with the gospel itself."

After this testimony of Prof. Harnack, it scarcely seems necessary to
cite other witnesses. He says of the early faith in the nearness of Christ's
second advent, and the establishing His reign of glory on the earth, "it
might be questioned whether it ought not to be regarded as an essential
part of the Christian religion," and "it was associated—to all appearance
inseparably associated—with the gospel itself." He would make no such
statement unless compelled to do so by the facts, and no man will dispute
his authority.

Neander, referring to the faith of the early Christians that the church
would come forth triumphant out of its conflicts, says, "They could at
first, as we have before remarked, conceive of it no otherwise than this,
that the struggle between the church and the pagan state would endure
till the triumph brought about from without, *by the return of Christ to
Judgement*" (Vol. I, p. 650).

Mosheim, referring to the controversies in the time of Origen, says, "Long before this period an opinion had prevailed that Christ was to come and reign a thousand years among men, before the entire and final dissolution of this world. *This opinion, which had hitherto met with no opposition*," etc. (Vol. I, p. 89).

Hagenbach, says, "The disciples of Christ, having received from their Master the promise of His second coming (parousia), the first Christians looked upon this event as near at hand, in connection with the general resurrection of the dead and the final Judgment."

Dorner says, as quoted in Hagenbach's *History of Doctrines*, "The Christian hope in the Christ that was to come grew out of faith in the Christ, who had already come," and adds, "Justin, writing at the time of Papias, says that it was *the general faith of all orthodox Christians*, and that only Gnostics did not share it."

Giesler, also quoted by Hagenbach, says of the first two centuries, "In all the works of this period *millenarianism is so prominent*, we cannot hesitate to consider it as universal in an age when such sensuous motives were certainly not unnecessary to animate men to suffer for Christianity" (Vol. I, p. 215).

Dr. Schaff says, in his *History of the Christian Church*, "The most striking point in the eschatology of the ancient church is the widely current and very prevalent chiliasm, or the doctrine of a visible reign of Christ in glory on the earth with the risen saints for a thousand years" (Vol. I, p. 299).

Bishop Renshaw says, "The commonly received opinion of a spiritual millennium, consisting in a universal triumph of the gospel, and the conversion of all nations for a thousand years before the coming of Christ, is a novel doctrine, unknown to the church for the space of sixteen hundred years."

Prof. Fisher, in *The Beginnings of Christianity*, says:

> "We call attention to the hopes and expectations of the apostles respecting the Second Advent of Christ, as they are disclosed in the New Testament writings.... This ex-

pectation is expressed by all apostles in terms which fairly
admit of no other interpretation. It is found in Paul (Rom
13:11–12; 1 Cor 7:29, 31; 10:11; Phil 4:5; 1 Tim 6:14);
… The same expectation is expressed in the Epistle to the
Hebrews (Heb 10:25, 37); in the Epistle of James (5:3, 8);
in the Epistles of Peter (1 Pet 4:7; 2 Pet 3:3); in the Epistle
of Jude (v. 18); in the first Epistle of John (2:18); and in
the Apocalypse (1:1; 3:2; 22:7, 12, 20). To put any other
construction on these passages, as if the Parousia to which
they refer, were anything else than the Second Advent
of the Lord to Judgment, would introduce a dangerous
license in interpretation, and one which might be employed to subvert the principal doctrines of the Christian
System."

But surely it is useless to quote further. If anything can be established
by human testimony, it is the fact that those who are looking for the
personal coming of the Lord, not for the conversion of the world by the
church, are in sympathy with the belief and teaching of the apostles and
early Christians. No one probably would be bold enough to deny that
such was the faith of the disciples, who were considered "Orthodox,"
for three hundred years, a period that has never been equaled in the
endurance of suffering for Christ's sake, and in the activity of missionary
zeal.

Coming to a later period, we find Prof. Briggs, utterly and fatally
wrong about the word of God, but able and scholarly, instructing the
Presbyterians with regard to the doctrine of their Confession of Faith.

"The current doctrine of a millennium in the future before the advent of Christ is another extra-confessional
doctrine, for which there is no basis in the Westminster
Standards. The Standards express the faith of the universal
catholic church in looking forward to the advent of Christ
for the judgment of the risen (?) world as imminent.…

The current doctrine is one for which Daniel Whitby, the Arminian [he should have added, the Arian], and the great revival of Methodism are chiefly responsible.... When recent Presbyterian divines go further, and adopt the scheme of the Arminian Whitby, they take a position which suits quite well with evangelical Methodism, but which is not in accord with Calvinism. They moreover go against the Scriptures, which do not recognize any such future millennium as this theory professes.

The doctrine of a future millennium is not so innocent as it appears to be on the surface. It changes the faith of the church in the imminency of the second advent of Christ. It makes the millennium the great hope of the future, instead of the presence of the Redeemer Himself. The Messiah is the great hope of the church, the supreme object of our living and striving, the Bridegroom for whose presence the affianced bride prays and agonizes. But the current theology pushes the Messiah behind the millennium, and fixes the hope of men upon an illusion and a delusion of human conceit and folly."

But as many are consciously or unconsciously influenced by the prevailing sentiment about them, it may be well to name some prominent men who are prominent premillennialists, although one who is not brave and independent enough to do his own thinking, apart from the prevailing sentiment of the time and country in which he lives, is hardly worth the trouble to help him into the light. He will be of little account, no matter on which side he at last elects to cast his lot. It was considered an unanswerable argument by the Pharisees, when Christ came the first time, to ask, "Have any of the rulers or of the Pharisees believed on Him?" (John 7:48). So several postmillennialists have recently asked concerning His second coming, either in stupid ignorance or willful prevarication, and it is of importance to show that the premillennialists are not wanting in scholars, expositors and preachers of the finest ability, as the world would say.

A brother, who is thoroughly familiar with modern German literature, asserts that "there is scarcely an expositor of any note on the Continent of Europe, who is not an avowed premillennialist," and adds, "let us rejoice that the best criticism, and Biblical as well as ecclesiastical and theological scholars such as Yan Oosterzee, Christlieb, Volck, Martensen, Weiss, Philippi, Koch, Grau, Olshausen, Christiani, Godet, have put postmillennialism and figurativism under their feet." He follows this with a long list of names as Bengel, Roos, Crusius, Hofman, Delitzsch, Auberlen, Lange, Luthardt, Koslin, Stier, DaCosta, Cappadose, Gaussen, and many others, eminent for their learning, who utterly reject the postmillennial heresy, and maintain the premillennial coming of our Lord. This is sometimes called the "continental view," but no matter whether it is continental or insular, so it is the truth of God.

In Great Britain we have such expositors as Alford, Ellicott, Fausset, Tregelles, Greswell, the Bishop of Liverpool. Among the Baptists we have such preachers as C. H. Spurgeon, H. Grattan Guinness, Archibald Brown, Frank White, and Henry Varley. Among the Presbyterians we have Dr. Horatius Bonar, Dr. Andrew Bonar, Dr. W. P. Mackay, Dr. Adolph Saphir, Dr. Sinclair Patterson, Dr. Donald Frazer, and John Wilkinson. The Church of England is represented by men such as Rev. Prebendary Auriol, Very Rev. Dean Fremantle, Rev. Marcus Rainsford, Rev. Canon Hoare, Rev. H. E. Brooke, Rev. H. W. WebbPeploe, Rev. C. Skrine, Rev. C. J. Goodhart, Rev. Burlington Wale, and Rev. J. Stevenson. Additionally, the Earl of Shaftesbury, the Earl of Cavan, Lord Radstock, and Sir Arthur Blackwood; to say nothing of the entire number of "Brethren" like J. N. Darby, William Kelly, C. H. McIntosh, William Lincoln, J. Denham Smith, J. Hudson Taylor, T. Shuldham Henry, B. W. Newton, I. B. Baines, and Arthur Pridham, embracing some of the most thorough scholars and some of the profoundest students of the Bible in the world. All of these, and scores of others who might be named have spoken and written much in defense of our Lord's premillennial coming.

In the United States it is sufficient to remind the reader that a premillennial conference was recently held in Brooklyn, called by one hundred and fifty Baptist ministers. Or it may be sufficient to mention the names of some who spoke at the premillennial conferences in New York and Chicago, or expressed hearty sympathy with the doctrine. From the Episcopal church, Bishop Vail, of Kansas, Bishop Baldwin, of Canada, Bishop Nicholson, of Philadelphia, Dr. S. H. Tyng, Dr. L. W. Bancroft, Dr. R. Newton, Dr. J. F. Grammer. From the Presbyterian church, Prof. J. D. Cooper, Prof. D. C. Marquis, Prof. W. G. Moorehead, Prof. J. T. Duffield, Prof. S. H. Kellogg, Dr. N. West, Dr. E. R. Craven, Dr. H. M. Parsons, Dr. William Dinwiddle, Dr. W. Erdman, Dr. Albert Erdman, Dr. J. F. Kendall, Dr. C. K. Imbrie, Dr. A. T. Pierson. From the Methodists, Prof. H. Lummis, Prof. E. F. Stroeter, Dr. James S. Kennedy, Wm. E. Blackstone. From the Baptists, Dr. A. J. Gordon, Dr. A. J. Frost, Dr. F. L. Chapell, Dr. H. M. Saunders, Robert Cameron. From the Congregationalists, Dr. E. P. Goodwin, Dr. H. D. Burton, Dr. Geo. F. Pentecost. From the Reformed Dutch, Dr. W. P. Gordon, Dr. Geo. S. Bishop, Dr. Rufus W. Clark. From the Lutherans, Dr. Joseph A. Seiss, Dr. Geo. N. H. Peters. And Evangelists like Moody, Munhall, Needham, Whittle; while hundreds more could be mentioned, if necessary.

It is a great mistake to suppose that premillennialists are but an insignificant company of cranks. They may be cranks, and it is well that they are in these days of infidelity among the professors and preachers, but they are loyal to our Lord Jesus Christ, and true to His word. There are thousands and tens of thousands of them in Europe and America, including the first men of the church in intellectual endowments, scholastic attainments, fervent piety, faithful service and intimate acquaintance with the Scriptures. Indeed it is the study of the Scriptures, which has led to such a remarkable revival of the old and true faith in the premillennial coming of our Lord. Just as this is written, a letter is received from a pastor in North Dakota, who says:

"For some time it has been my purpose to procure a lot of
suitable books, and investigate the subject of the Second
Advent of Christ. But, my dear brother, I had the book
I needed at hand. It was the BIBLE. Taking that as 'the
Supreme Judge, by which all controversies of religion are
to be determined,' I went at it with an honest desire to
know the truth. Need I say more? You know where such
work must end."

Premillennialists, however misrepresented or misunderstood, can always sing the song of Moses, when brought to face those who reject
the truth: "Their rock is not as our Rock, even our enemies themselves
being judges" (Deut 32:31). By far the ablest book that has ever appeared
against the truth was written by Dr. David Brown, already frequently
mentioned in these pages. To a premillennialist, the admissions he makes
are very remarkable from his stand point, and would have been all that
can be demanded, if he had not spoiled them by contradictory statements.

"Premillennialists have done the church a real service, by
calling attention to the place which the second advent
holds in the word of God and the scheme of divine truth.
If the controversy which they have raised should issue in a
fresh and impartial inquiry into this branch of it, I for one,
instead of regretting, shall rejoice in the agitation of it.
When they dilate upon the prominence given to this doctrine in scripture, and the practical uses which are made
of it, they touch a chord in the heart of every simple lover
of his Lord, and carry conviction to all who tremble at
His word.... With them we affirm that the REDEEMER'S
SECOND APPEARING IS THE VERY POLE-STAR
OF THE CHURCH [the capitals are his own]. That it is
so held forth in the New Testament is beyond dispute."

He tells us "there are certain minds which, either from constitutional temperament, or the particular school of theology to which they are attached, have tendencies in the direction of premillennialism so strong that they are ready to embrace it almost immediately *con amore*." But what sort of minds are they? Cranky, curious, credulous? Nay, verily.

> "Souls that burn with love to Christ, who with the mother of Sisera, cry through the lattice, 'Why is his chariot so long in coming? Why tarry the wheels of His chariots?' and with the spouse, 'Make haste, my Beloved, and be Thou like to a roe, or a young hart upon the mountains of spices'—such souls are ready to catch at a doctrine which seems to promise a much earlier appearing of their beloved Lord than the ordinary view ... But are there no *anti*-premillennial tendencies which require to be guarded against? I think there are. Under the influence of such tendencies, the inspired text, as such presents no rich and exhaustless field of prayerful and delighted investigation; exegetical inquiries and discoveries are an uncongenial element; and whatever scripture intimations regarding the future destinies of the church and of the world involve events out of the usual range of human occurrences, or exceeding the anticipations of enlightened Christian sagacity, are almost instinctively overlooked or softened down."

One would think it well to be found in the first of those two companies, not in the second, especially since Dr. Brown assures us that we should never be satisfied with anything less than the personal coming of our Lord.

> "Would it be incongruous in the church to mourn and feel desolate in the *presence* of her Lord? Not less incongruous, it seems, is it *not* to cherish the feeling of desolation in His

absence. And both are such incongruities as confounding
the seasons of fasting and feasting, as putting a piece of
new garment upon an old, as putting new wine into old
bottles, and preferring new wine to old.... Jesus will think
it an abuse of His consolations if we have learned from
them to do without Him. Written communications and
tokens of affection from the absent One are dear to affection—but only when Himself cannot be had. Christ's
word, and the seals of His love conveyed to our hearts
by the blessed Spirit, are inexpressibly dear to His loving
people—but only in the absence of Himself. And never
do we please Christ so much as when we 'refuse to be
comforted,' even with His own consolations, save in the
prospect of *His Personal Return* [emphasis Brown's]."

But let it not be imagined that the truth, although supported by divine
authority and sustained by human authority, will prevail "till He come."
Only a line of witnesses to the blessed hope will be kept up, and this is
all. The apostasy has set in and has come to stay. Of course God could
revive His "work in the midst of the years, in the midst of the years make
known, in wrath remember mercy," and if it please the Lord still to tarry,
this He must do, or "all will come to desolation." Quite a number of
godly men, who are postmillennialists, clearly see and deeply deplore
the wretched condition of the professing Christian body, and frankly
confess that the extraordinary manifestation of divine grace and power is
absolutely necessary to save from impending ruin, and to call the church
back to the gospel. But the probability is very great that we are hemmed
in by the perils of the last days, and hence the witnesses can do nothing
more in the midnight darkness than to cry, "Behold the Bridegroom
cometh" (Matt 25:6).

"Bride of the Lamb, awake! awake!
Why sleep for sorrow now?
The hope of glory, Christ, is thine,
An heir of glory thou.
Thy spirit, through the lonely night,
From earthly joy apart,
Hath sigh'd for one that's far away—
The Bridegroom of thy heart.

But see, the night is waning fast,
The breaking morn is near;
And Jesus comes, with voice of love,
Thy drooping heart to cheer.
He comes—for, oh! His yearning heart
No more can bear delay—
To scenes of full unmingled joy
To call His Bride away.

Thou, too, shalt reign—He will not wear
His crown of joy alone!
And earth His royal Bride shall see
Beside Him on the throne.
Then weep no more—'tis all thine own—
His crown, His joy divine,
And, sweeter far than all beside,
He, He himself is thine."

14

The Order of Events

"When the Most High divided to the nations their inheritance, when he separated the sons of Adam, He set the bounds of the people according to the number of the children of Israel" (Deut 32:8). Perhaps most professing Christians would hear with a smile of derision or incredulity, that, in the distribution of the earth's surface among various nationalities, He had special reference to a people so few and despised as the Jews, and not to the great powers, like the Grecian, Roman, Russian, German, and British empires, and the proud Republic of the United States. Nevertheless it is a fact, and a fact we will do well to keep in mind when we search the Scriptures of truth.

It was to the Jews He said, "Ye have seen what I did unto the Egyptians, and how I bare you on eagles' wings, and brought you unto myself. Now therefore, if ye will obey my voice indeed, and keep my covenant, then ye shall be a peculiar treasure unto me above all people: for all the earth is mine, and ye shall be unto me a kingdom of priests, and a holy nation" (Exod 19.4–6). Alas! Scarcely had "all the people answered with one voice, and said, All the words which the Lord hath said will we do," ratifying the covenant with blood, before they sneered at Moses, and made them a molten calf to worship (cf. Exod 24:3–8; 32:1–4). From that time and onward, their history was stained with disobedience, idolatry, unbelief and worldliness, until infinite patience could endure no longer, and they were disowned and rejected, and scattered among the nations of the earth.

In the year 722 before Christ, the ten tribes that had revolted from the house of David under Solomon's successor were carried away to Assyria, and the land was possessed by other people. In the year 586 before Christ, Jerusalem was destroyed by Nebuchadnezzar, and to this day remains under the hand of its Gentile masters.[1] Hence, for 2500 years Israel has been the nation without a home, the nation of weary foot like the Wandering Jew, the nation which even professedly Christian nations have delighted to persecute and torture. For nearly eighteen hundred years after the Son of God came into the world, kings and cabinets, pretending at least to have some regard for His teachings, have inflicted upon the hated descendants of Abraham, and Isaac, and Jacob banishment, extortion, oppression, outrage, murder, and all manner of cruelty. Even now, at the close of the nineteenth century, with its boasted civilization and progress, Russia, Romania, Bulgaria, Germany, and many other peoples think it right to molest and rob, and exile, and kill a Jew.

> "The wild dove hath its nest, the fox its cave,
> Mankind its country, Israel but the grave."

The same inspired and infallible word, however, which plainly and frequently predicts their dispersion and punishment, just as plainly and much more frequently predicts their restoration to their own land, when and where they shall look upon Him whom they pierced, and at last accept Him as their long-promised Messiah (cf. Zech 12:10). No Christian who believes that "the prophecy came not in old time [or at any time] by the will of man; but holy men of God spake as they were moved by the Holy Ghost" (2 Pet 1:21), can have a shadow of doubt concerning the future gathering of the now scattered Israelites into their own country, if he also believes that the Holy Ghost said what he meant, and meant what He said.

Meanwhile "the times of the Gentiles" set in when Israel was set aside, and Babylon was the head of the new order of things described in the

---

1. While true at the time in 1891 when Brookes wrote this, in 1967 Israel regained complete control over Jerusalem.

prophecy through Daniel. It is remarkable that from near the beginning of the second chapter to the close of the seventh, the Holy Ghost writes in the Chaldee language,[2] as if He would say to the Gentiles, read in your own vernacular the characteristic features of your times and your fearful fall. Daniel 2 shows us Gentile estimate of governmental power, as seen in the stately image of Nebuchadnezzar's dream. Daniel 3 shows us Gentile ambition, as seen in the golden image, reared nineteen years later by the king of Babylon. Daniel 4 shows us Gentile pride saying, "Is not this great Babylon that I have built?" and then degraded to the level of the beasts in the person of the boastful king. Daniel 5 shows us Gentile impiety and revelry and sensuality, profaning the sacred vessels of God's house, until the fingers of a man's hand wrote its doom over against the candlestick upon the wall of the king's palace. Daniel 6 shows us Gentile blasphemy, making man an object of worship, as in the days of the Antichrist. Daniel 7 shows us Gentile persecution of the saints, under the Antichrist, until Jesus comes.

In other words, dominion or government in the hands of Gentiles will prove as complete a failure as it did in the hands of the Israelites; and if it be said that we have in this age the word of God, and the presence of the Spirit to restrain men from evil, let us not forget what was written concerning His people in former times; "Yea, they made their hearts as an adamant stone, lest they should hear the law, and the words which the Lord of hosts sent by His Spirit through the former prophets: therefore came a great wrath from the Lord of hosts" (Zech 7:12). Men sin against more light and mercy in our day, and therefore will be held to a stricter accountability and overtaken by a sorer punishment.

It has been previously shown by the sure testimony of God that the present age must close in universal apostasy and lawlessness. It shall be as when the flood came and destroyed them all. It shall be as when Lot was hurried out of Sodom. Antichrist shall be manifested in all his blasphemy and malignant hatred of the true Christ. "In the last days perilous times shall come" (2 Tim 3:1). Perhaps no religious book printed during the

---

2. Aramaic was often called the Chaldee language in past scholarship.

present generation has received more universal approval than Bernard's *Progress of Doctrine in the New Testament.*

Dr. Alvah Hovey, of the Newton Theological Institution, who introduced it to the American public, said, "The Bampton Lectures of Mr. Bernard on the Progress of Doctrine in the New Testament, deserve unqualified commendation, for they are as nearly perfect, both in substance and form, as any human production can well be made."

This, no doubt, expresses the view of intelligent ministers and Christians of all denominations; for no one, so far as known, has been found to dissent from its statements. It is well, therefore, to read attentively what this remarkable expositor has to say concerning the end of our dispensation.

> "I know not how any man, in closing the Epistles, could expect to find the subsequent history of the Church essentially different from what it is. In those writings we seem, as it were, not to witness some passing storms which clear the air, but to feel the whole atmosphere charged with the elements of future tempest and death. Every moment the forces of evil show themselves more plainly. They are encountered, but not dissipated. Or, to change the figure, we see battles fought by the leaders of our band, but no security is promised by their victories. New assaults are being prepared; new tactics will be tried; new enemies pour on; the distant hills are black with gathering multitudes, and the last exhortations of those who fall at their posts call on their successors to 'endure hardness as good soldiers of Jesus Christ,' and 'earnestly to contend for the faith which was once delivered to the saints.'
>
> The fact which I observe is not merely that these indications of the future are in the Epistles, but that they increase as we approach the close, and after the doctrines of the Gospel have been fully wrought out, and the fullness

of personal salvation and the ideal character of the church
has been placed in the clearest light, the shadows gather
and deepen on the external history. The last words of St.
Paul in the second Epistle to Timothy, and those of St.
Peter in his second Epistle, with the Epistles of St. John
and St. Jude, breathe the language of a time in which
the tendencies of that history had distinctly shown themselves; and in this respect these writings form a prelude
and a passage to the Apocalypse."

Of the general meaning of the Apocalypse he writes truly as follows,
the italics being his own:

"The book is a doctrine of the power and *coming* of our
Lord Jesus Christ, 'Behold he cometh with clouds, and
every eye shall see him.' That is the first voice, and the
keynote of the whole. The Epistles to the Seven Churches
(symbolical representatives of the whole Church in its
various conditions) all take their tone from this thought,
and are the voice of a Lord who will 'come quickly.' The
visions which follow draw to the same end, and the last
voices of the book respond to the first, and attest its
subject and its purpose. 'He which testifieth these things
saith, surely I come quickly. Amen. Even so, come, Lord
Jesus.' Whatever else the Christian desires is bound up
in this prospect. The deliverance of the creation from its
present groans and travail, the redemption of our body,
the perfection of man in a holy community, and the re-
alization in outward things of the tendencies of the renewed nature, all these hopes wait on the one hope of *His*
appearing."

If this is so, and perhaps none will dispute it, how strange it seems that
the hope of His appearing has no place in the thought or discourse of a

vast majority of Christians! Men speak of dying and going to heaven, but how few of the coming of the Lord? Such indifference is no doubt due to the artifice of Satan, who, as Calvin says, "in plucking up the faith of Christ's coming, aims directly at the throat of the church." It is not death that is set before us, horrible death, loathsome death, with its frequent preliminary agonies and pangs and tortures, that make the suffering of a martyr by fire as nothing in comparison, but it is the coming of the Lord to destroy death. Dr. James Culross, the author of many valuable books, and one of the ablest of English writers, has well expressed the truth on this subject:

> "No reflecting man can think lightly of death or drive it from his contemplation. But in our religious speech we have too often placed it where the Bible does not place it, and have caused it to intercept and in a measure hide from view the coming of the Lord. Taking what we find in the New Testament, the true Christian attitude is that of waiting for the Lord from heaven.... He is to return in power and great glory, having received the Kingdom. There is nothing that meets us more distinctly and largely in the New Testament than this. We cannot 'spiritualize' it. We may as well 'spiritualize' His resurrection and ascension.... It is not merely that prophets and apostles have told us of His return; He has done so Himself, and that not merely by way of bare prediction or intimation of his purpose, but by way of *promise*. Were He not to return He would break his word. The promise meets us again and again, and in the greatest variety of form."

First, He will come in person. "This same Jesus, which is taken up from you into heaven, shall so come in like manner, as ye have seen Him go into heaven" (Acts 1:11). "The Lord Himself shall descend from heaven with a shout" (1 Thess 4:16). This does not mean an angel, nor the Holy Spirit, nor death, nor any providential event whatever, but

the Lord Jesus Christ Himself, who summons His own believing and
saved ones to meet Him, "that every one may receive the things done
through his body" (2 Cor 5:10); that He may "know how much every
man had gained by trading" (Luke 19:15); that He may "give every man
according as his work shall be" (Rev 22:12). With this judgment scene
the unbelieving world has nothing to do, but only the saints who are
assigned their position in the kingdom according to their faithfulness,
and of whom it is said, "Do ye not know that the saints shall judge the
world?" (1 Cor 6:2).

Second, He may come at any day, for there is no predicted event that
awaits fulfillment between this passing moment, and His coming for His
people to gather them about Himself in the air. The popular view that
the world is first to be converted is a most delusive dream, for which
there is not the slightest warrant in the word of God, in the history of
the church, or in the present outlook. The view probably arose from
the hideous lie of evolution, it being assumed that there is an inherent
tendency in human nature to reach a higher development, or, as poor
Beecher used to say, after he became an evolutionist and infidel, "man
has been failing upward ever since his creation." If this is true, and the
evil and vulgar beast has made no nobler attainment than that which we
see at the close of the nineteenth century, he must have had a mighty low
start. His tendency is not toward a higher development in religion and
morals, but he will gravitate towards the devil, so that the last days will
be the worst days, as the Scriptures plainly teach.

Third, at the coming of the Lord *for* His saints there shall be a resurrection of all who "sleep in Jesus," and of none others: "Blessed and holy
is he that hath part in the first resurrection; on such the second death hath
no power, But they shall be priests of God and of Christ, and shall reign
with Him a thousand years" (Rev 20:6). The common interpretation,
that this refers to the revival of martyr principals, is a self-evident absur-
dity, for while we may think, in a figure of speech, of principals being
kings, or reigning, it is impossible to conceive of principals as priests
of God. Alford well says on these words, "Those who lived next to the
apostles, and the whole church for 300 years, understood them in the
plain, literal sense," and he adds, that unless so accepted, "there is an end

of all significance in language, and Scripture is wiped out as a definite testimony to anything."

Even if there is a simultaneous resurrection of the righteous and unrighteous at the coming of the Lord, there is the most marked difference between them, for only the former have bodies that are glorified, incorruptible, and shining in the likeness of the Redeemer. This is the resurrection for which Paul panted and strove, "the resurrection of the dead" (Phil 3:11); and it is unaccountable that the apostle earnestly desired, if by any means he might attain unto a resurrection common to all, and unavoidable. So our Lord tells us about "the resurrection of the just" (Luke 14:14); and speaks of those who "shall be accounted worthy to obtain that world, and the resurrection from the dead" (Luke 20:35), or "the resurrection which is from among the dead," as Rotherham properly renders it. Even the Old Testament teaches this elective resurrection, peculiar to the saints, when it says, "Many of them that sleep in the dust of the earth shall awake, these [that awake] to everlasting life, and those [that awake not] to shame and everlasting contempt" (Dan 12:2). In the great New Testament chapters which treat the resurrection, not a word is said concerning the resurrection of the unbelievers, but only of the saints (cf. 1 Cor 15; 1 Thess 4:13–18). Surely "there shall be a resurrection of the dead, both of the just and the unjust" (Acts 20:15); but only of the just at the coming of Christ. "But the rest of the dead lived not again until the thousand years were finished" (Rev 20:5).

Fourth, the true church, the regenerated ones, having been caught away, a foul and apostate religious system will be left, associated with the Antichrist, whose rise and progress are symbolized in the seal judgments of the Apocalypse, the first three and a half years of his reign in the trumpet judgments, and the last three and a half years in the vial [bowl] judgments, the overthrow of Babylon, or all that exalts itself against God, both in its ecclesiastical and political aspect, being depicted in the seventeenth and eighteenth chapters of that marvelous book. The Jews shall have been partially restored to their own land in unbelief, and there pass through the great tribulation, such as was not since the beginning of the world, when the Lord Jesus Christ will suddenly appear with all His saints, to deliver His people from their distress, to cast the Antichrist and the false prophet alive into the lake of fire burning with brimstone, and to establish His millennial kingdom (Zech 14:1–5; Rev 19:16–21).

Fifth, when He appears again in the midst of Israel, when He builds again the tabernacle of David, which is fallen down (Joel 2:27–32; Acts 15:16–17), then shall He pour out His Spirit upon all flesh, and the knowledge of His glory shall flood the earth, as the waters cover the sea (Hab 2:14). In that day, and not before:

- "the inhabitant shall not say, I am sick; the people that dwell therein shall be forgiven their iniquity" (Isa 33:24).

- "Thy people also shall be all righteous: they shall inherit the land forever, the branch of my planting, the work of my hands, that I may be glorified" (Isa 60:21).

- "and they shall teach no more every man his neighbor, and every man his brother, saying, Know the Lord; for they shall all know me, from the least of them unto the greatest of them, saith the Lord; for I will forgive their iniquity, and I will remember their sin no more" (Jer 31:34).

- "And the Lord shall be King over all the earth: in that day shall there be one Lord, and His name one" (Zech 14:9).

Sixth, when the thousand years are expired, Satan shall be loosed out of his prison, the bottomless abyss in which he has been bound during the millennium, and shall go out to deceive the nations, in a last desperate effort to thwart the counsels of God. But he shall not succeed, for he shall be cast into the lake of fire and brimstone, where the Antichrist and false prophet are, his seventh and final defeat and fall (Rev 20:7–10). After the judgment of the great white throne, death and hades, thank God, shall be cast into the lake of fire. But what a picture does this give to us of the mind of the flesh, that, even after the blessedness and the glory of the millennial reign, it can be corrupted, and lift itself again in insolent defiance of divine authority and infinite love.

Seventh, eternity begins.

"And God shall wipe away all tears from their eyes; and there shall be no more death, neither sorrow, nor crying, neither shall there be any more pain: for the former things are passed away.... And there shall be no more curse: but the throne of God and the Lamb shall be in it; and His servants shall serve Him: and they shall see His face; and His name shall be in their foreheads. And there shall be no night there: and they need no candle, neither light of the sun; for the Lord God giveth them light: and they shall reign for ever and ever.... He which testifieth these things saith, Surely I come quickly. Amen. Even so, come, Lord Jesus" (Rev 21:4; 22:3–5, 20).

"I am waiting for the dawning
Of the bright and blessed day;
When the darksome night of sorrow
Shall have vanished far away:
When forever with the Saviour,
Far beyond this vale of tears,
I shall swell the song of worship
Through the everlasting years.

I am looking at the brightness,
(See, it shineth from afar),
Of the clear and joyous beaming,
Of the "Bright and Morning Star";
Through the dark grey mist of morning
Do I see its glorious light;
Then away with every shadow
Of this sad and weary night.

I am waiting for the coming
Of the Lord who died for me:
Oh! His words have thrilled my spirit,
"I will come again for thee."
I can almost hear His footfall
On the threshold of the door,
And my heart, my heart is longing
To be His for evermore."

Amen! Maranatha!

www.ingramcontent.com/pod-product-compliance
Lightning Source LLC
Chambersburg PA
CBHW071154120626
46546CB00006B/2267